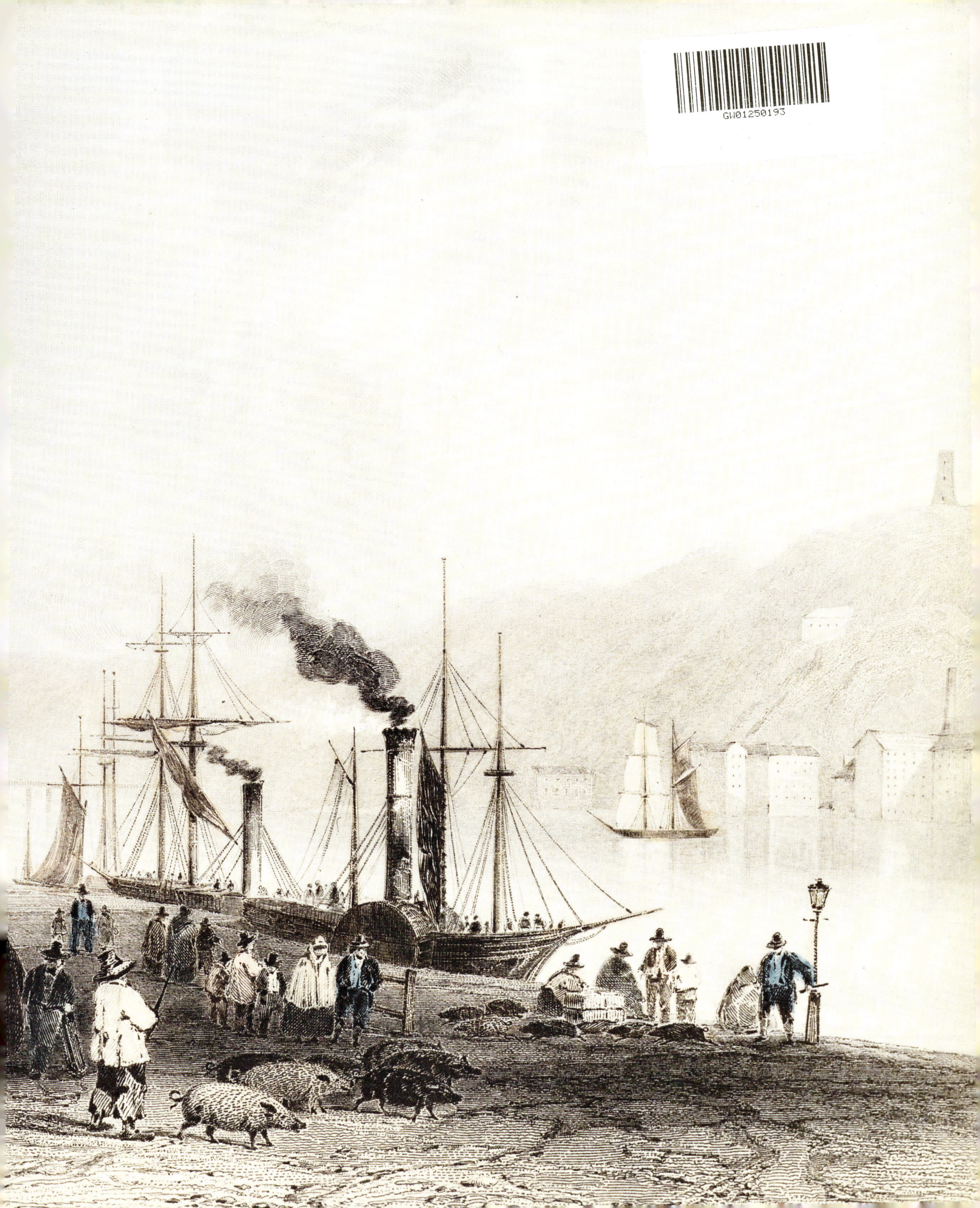

IRELAND

'I am of Ireland,
And the Holy Land of Ireland,
And time runs on,' cried she.
'Come out of charity,
Come dance with me in Ireland.'

W B Yeats

GILL & MACMILLAN

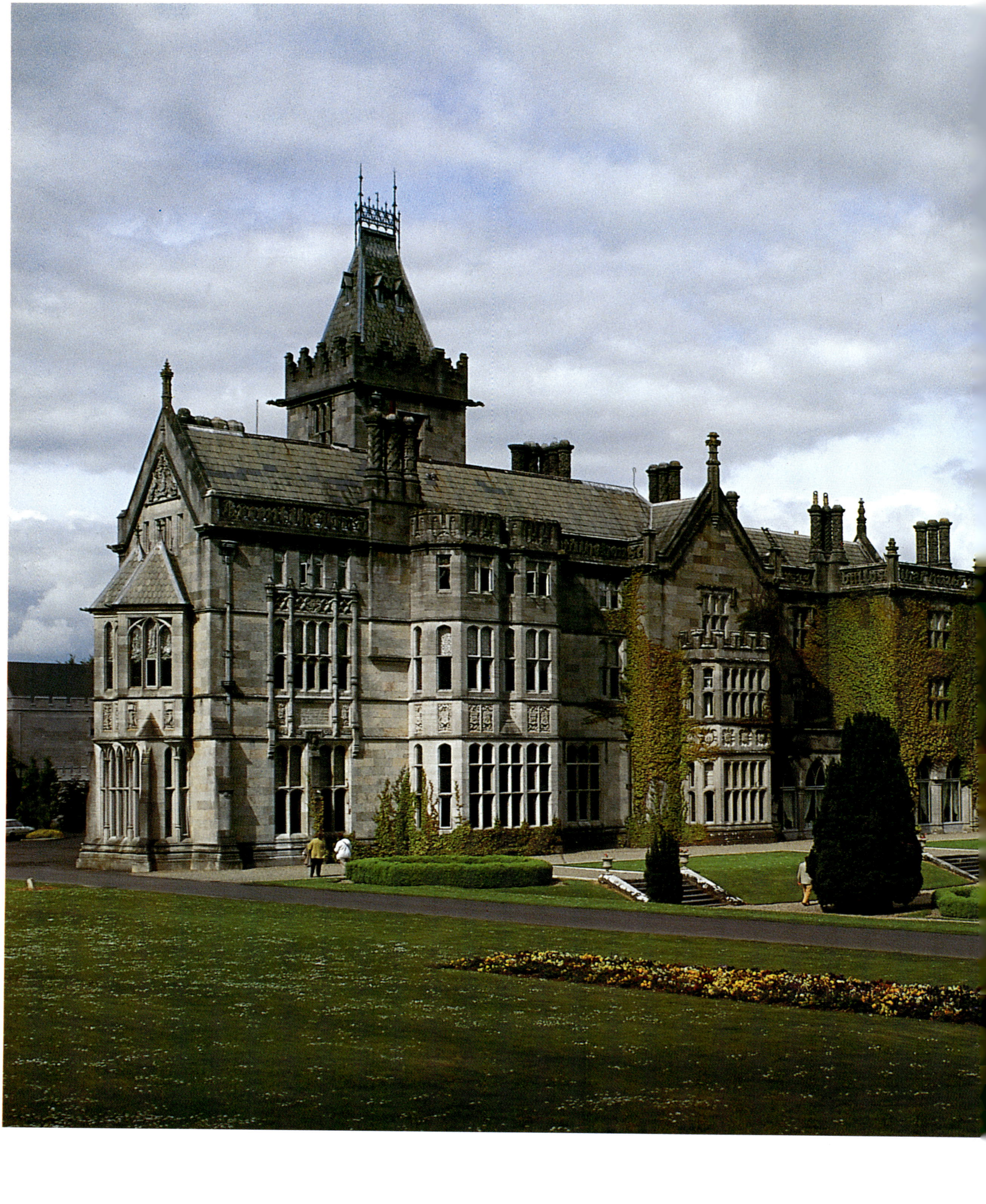

IRELAND

A Photographic Portrait

Introduction by J.P. Donleavy

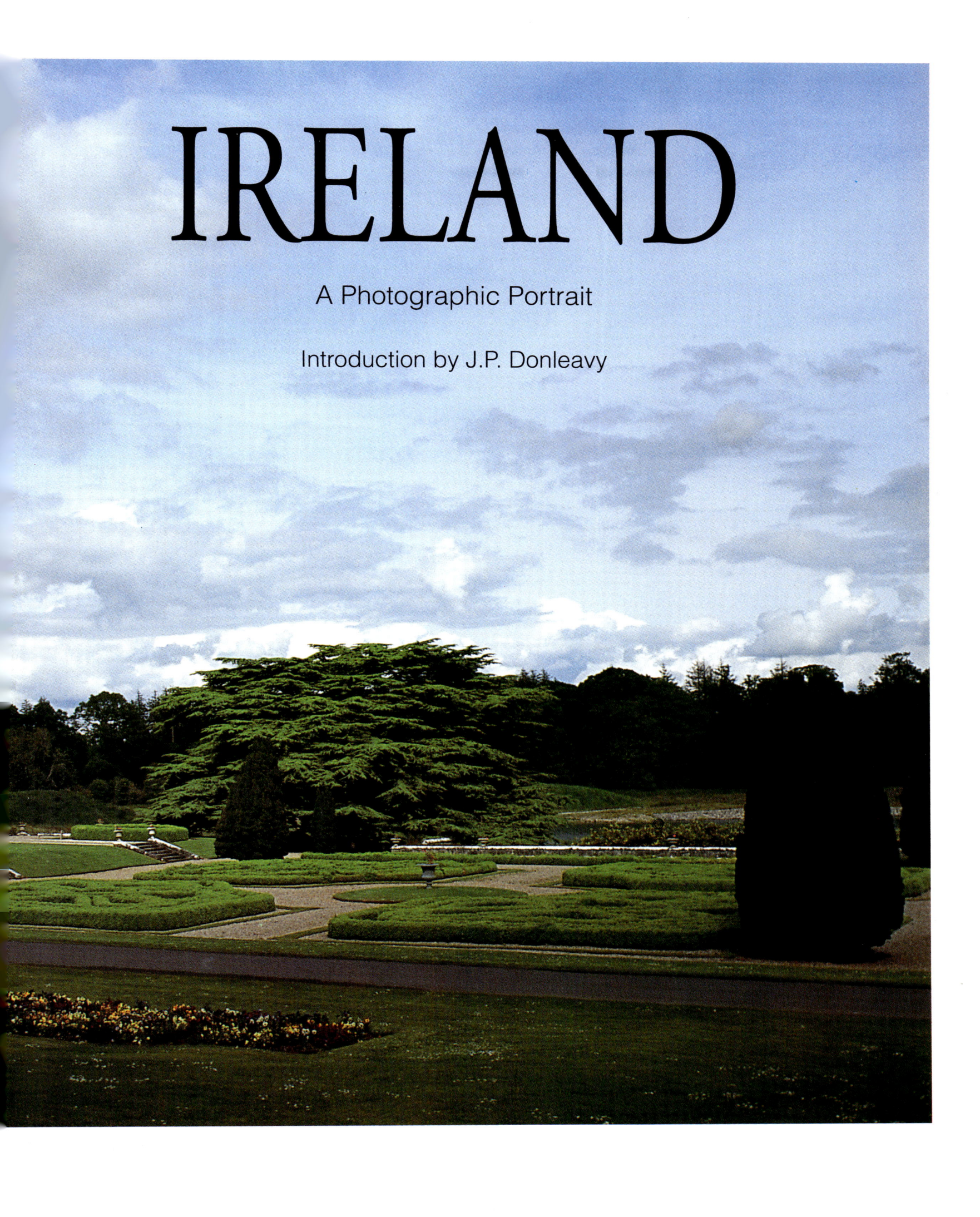

CONTENTS

The extraordinary island

Picture Section

Introduction by J.P. Donleavy	6	Sláinte	11
Dublin and the East	19	History	11
The South West with the Ring of Kerry	43	The faces of Ireland	16
The Loughs around the Shannon	67	The pub - an Irish institution	35
The West	85	Whiskey and black beer	37
Achill Island and the North West	109	Traditional and modern	35
Northern Ireland	136	Bed and Breakfast - An Irish Adventure	59

Right at the top of the hit parade: Folk music	61
Dublin	62
The Church - Religion in the past and today	64
Fishing in Ireland	66
Northern Ireland	75
Literature	77

Page 1: Irishmen from Cahirciveen.
Pages 2 and 3: Adare Manor Hotel, Adare
Above: Ruins of the Anglo-Norman Adare Abbey

TRAVEL GUIDE

Contents • A brief study of the area	101
Routes through Ireland : six suggestions	125
Route map	127
A to Z of tourist attractions and landscapes	131
In the land of betting and racing enthusiasts	134
Being a pleasure boat skipper on the Shannon	153
Map of Ireland	155
Index	156
Imprint	160

Introduction by J.P. Donleavy

I live here for my sins and for my tax-free status on earnings received from what I presently write and have already written. Not the worst arrangement, for many of my novels occur amid the scenes and settings ancient and modern vividly described by word and photograph in this handsome book. And this combination of strange factors will not be unfamiliar to others who have come here to reside for similar reasons. Full as Ireland is of its myths, leprechauns, blarney and blandishment. Such perhaps even verging on the mawkish as it is liberally doled out by its friendly welcoming people and the state bodies who represent them. But I still, after twenty-five years, have no intention of leaving.

In spite of its literary censorship, subjugation by a neighbouring island, its famed famine and long impoverishment, no country on the face of the earth has attached to it an amount of romantic imagery as has this emerald isle. And such kept burningly alive by those escaped and exported from Ireland over the years as emigrants to other distant climes and places. Leaving well behind them the 'crut', a chronic usually celibate condition of repression known to encumber the spirit, and leave its victim possessed with guilt and superstition which in turn had long to be kept in check and disguised by respectability and a deep devotion to religion. You might even say it was a place where friendship was on the lips but not in the heart. Because, if giving vent to honesty, the truth ever got out, the gossip then spreading about the impure, defiant and disreputable thoughts you were really thinking, would ruin you.

Ah but now, come up to date. Forget all this old rubbish about the true nature of the Irish. The thoughts in the mind might not have changed but this is a brand new place not only for the native but for the visitor. And you would be fearfully wrong to think that any of the above guilt and superstition, impure and disreputable thoughts, had anything to do with the modern Ireland of the present, awakened as it has been from its centuries of slumber. Yet the past flavours and forecasts the future. The ghost of the two decker green upholstered tram still rumbles its way through the heart of Dublin city. There it goes now with the half-dreaming poets aboard heading nowhere and everywhere and this versifier looking down at the passing citizens with a gimlet eye in case he should recognise someone, and could jump down, stop them in their tracks and borrow half a crown.

Gone too are the shouters who from the curbside would proclaim their theories as to origin of the stars. And no more are the massive draught horses and drays, barrels of Guinness aboard, clip clopping upon the roadway amid a swarm of cyclists, the white gloved hands of the seven-foot-tall Garda Siochana raised, starting and stopping the traffic. And woe betide the infractor of a rule. He'd soon be told to mind his manners and keep his wheels where they should be. Or if on foot to take the pair of his feet and to get back up on the curb and rejoin the alive life on the glistening granite pavements. That was the old Dublin of my university years.

But as has happened in the modern metropolis across the world, cities and towns are monitored by red and green lights and white striped pedestrian crossings. And plied by taxis, buses and crammed with motor cars. Even in Irish towns and cities, the worst has happened, the vehicle glut has dawned. But there is a difference. Crawling along you get a chance to see the architecture, not only in the buildings but also worn on the faces. Or in a taxi to be entertained by the astonishing erudition of the drivers. And no question you've got on your mind to ask will go unanswered. Indeed you might even detour and repair to a pub together to finish the discussion. But, of course, while the taxi meter outside is kept running tabulating up the fare.

Now from my unexpurgated opinions, you mustn't get the totally wrong blissful impression. As you won't. For you'll soon be reminded that the irascible, perverse and cantankerous are everywhere. And if you're a visitor, you'll be concluding that Ireland would be nearly just like the place you've just left. Except that as soon as you decided it was, you'd find out that it isn't. For out across this land there'd be plenty of conundrums. Safety of self, because it is thought to be in the hands of God, is still something many a native chooses to ignore. On wheels with a few jars of the wine of the country taken, a citizen coming around any blind bend like the hammers of hell, will not in any way be mindful that you may be coming around the same bend in the opposite direction. But not to worry. Ireland has the best of ambulances to take you to the most up to date of hospitals.

But one thing can never be denied and that is the general amiability and hospitality of the people. Reinforced by the numerous signs for bed and breakfast that you will see every few yards along the road from one coast to another. And what is to be had and found even in the most humble of homes, is both cheap and good. And for extra amusement you can also climb right up the social scale, motor up their mile long drive, step out on their vast apron of gravel, and be greeted by the titled and once high and mighty. Who will usher you into their castle, rubbing their hands in anticipation of monetary reward, while giving a tug or two at the forelock and treating you to the best brogue you've ever heard. For keeping the silverware shined and the roofs on some of these places would bankrupt you.

Now your next phenomenon is that on foot in Dublin or in any decent town, turn in any direction and you are never more than a hundred paces from a pint of stout and every refurbished pub or hotel has a room named after gentlemen whose photographs appear in this very book and who in previous times had their work banned and were driven away from these shores. Three of whom are James Joyce, Samuel Beckett and Brendan Behan. And appropriate enough in the latter's case, as it must be said, he, with insults quickly leading to mayhem, wrecked plenty of these places in his time. His favourite more peaceful antic being to take 'an anointing of the spirit' as he called it by pouring a pint of porter over his head. And to then give a rendition of a British judge sentencing him to death.

No matter how well you know it, Ireland, like the bright paint slapped up everywhere, will always come to you as a surprise. Famine once writ upon the soul of this island, and long lingering in its psyche is now nowhere to be seen or felt. Feast is the word everywhere as this nation so long torn by troubles and adversity, has none amounting to too much at the moment. The swarm of the recent generation of children, nicely American accented from television and non believing in religion, are two fisted and footed proclaiming their independence, and living life hanging on by their fingertips. Music and dancing is everywhere. And although the famed dungeon outpost of the Catacombs of my own time is gone, and where the inebriated dispossessed cavorted and great minds conferred, there still remains a social life, with none like it anywhere else in the world. And where the definition of clarity is still remembered as that force given to a fist that when sent in the direction of a face that when hit had no trouble seeing stars.

As you would imagine such dramatic changes in any nation with a past like Ireland's can cause a lot of publicity to go circulating around the world. And you guessed it, another new big surprise is in store. Word has finally reached the ears of the rich and famous who have heard news of this place on the edge of Europe with a bunch of marvellous international banks and tax advisors aplenty and these rich and famous are girding loins to make their assault. Descending out of the sky to restore the big mansions and castles with the best plumbing money can buy, mending the leaks in the roofs and re-animating the splendour that once reigned in the grand halls, drawing rooms and ballrooms. And to enjoy, if not their anonymity, at least their humility. For among the Irish you can wash off and shed your celebrity and be as natural and normal as other natural and normal human beings. As in Ireland, far away from the tumult and torture of crowded places, no one matters more than you do and no better place exists on earth to be with your own decent fair-minded self wrapped up in solitude.

And now what more can I say than the best words I ever said about Ireland which were the last words said in *The Ginger Man*. Come here till I tell you. Where is the sea high and the winds soft and moist and warm, sometimes stained with sun, with peace so wild for wishing where all is told and telling. On a winter night I heard horses on a country road, beating sparks out of the stones. I knew they were running away and would be crossing the fields where the pounding would come up into my ears. And I said they are running out to death which is with some soul and their eyes are mad and teeth out.

God's mercy
On the wild
Ginger Man
And on Ireland

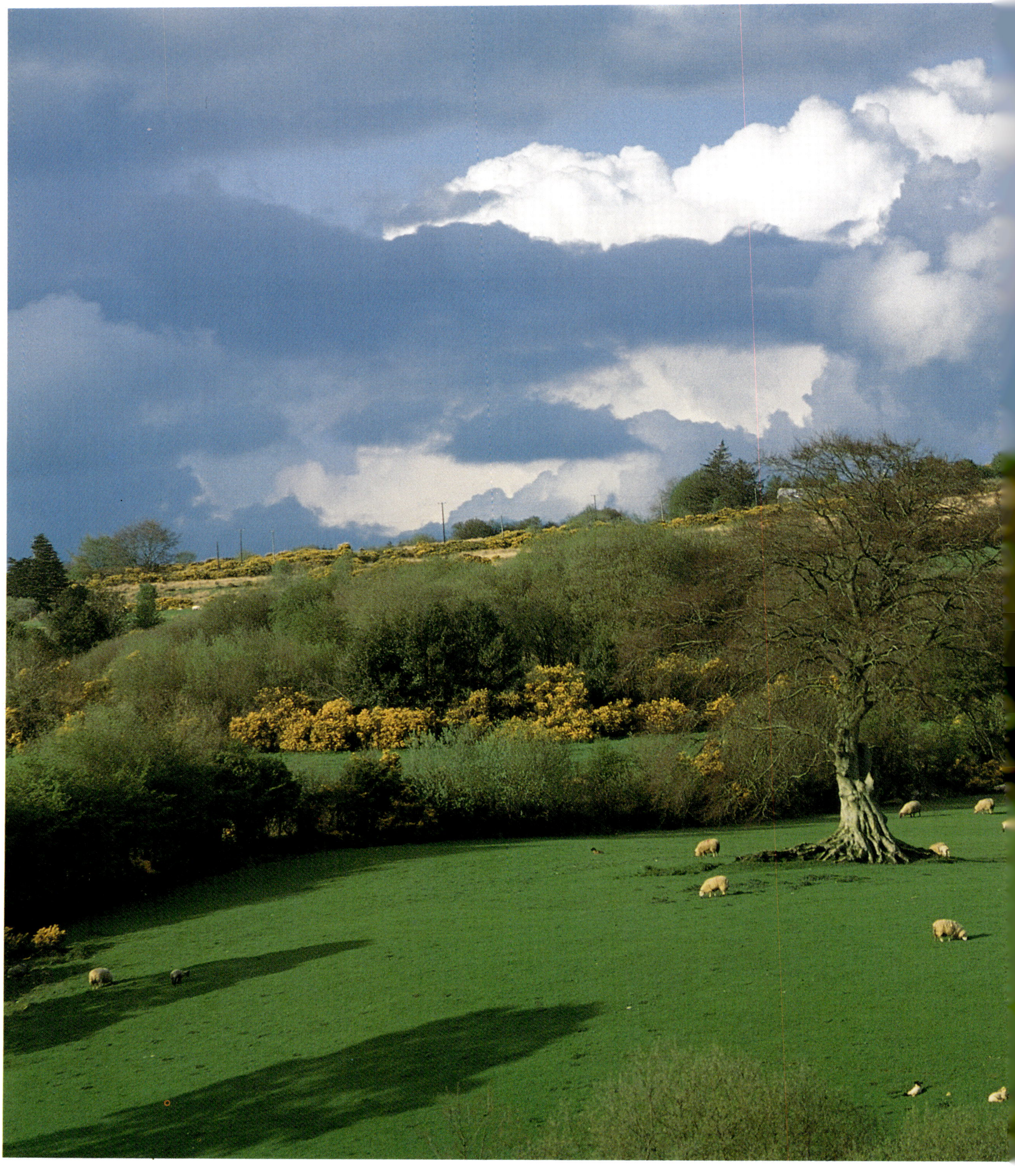

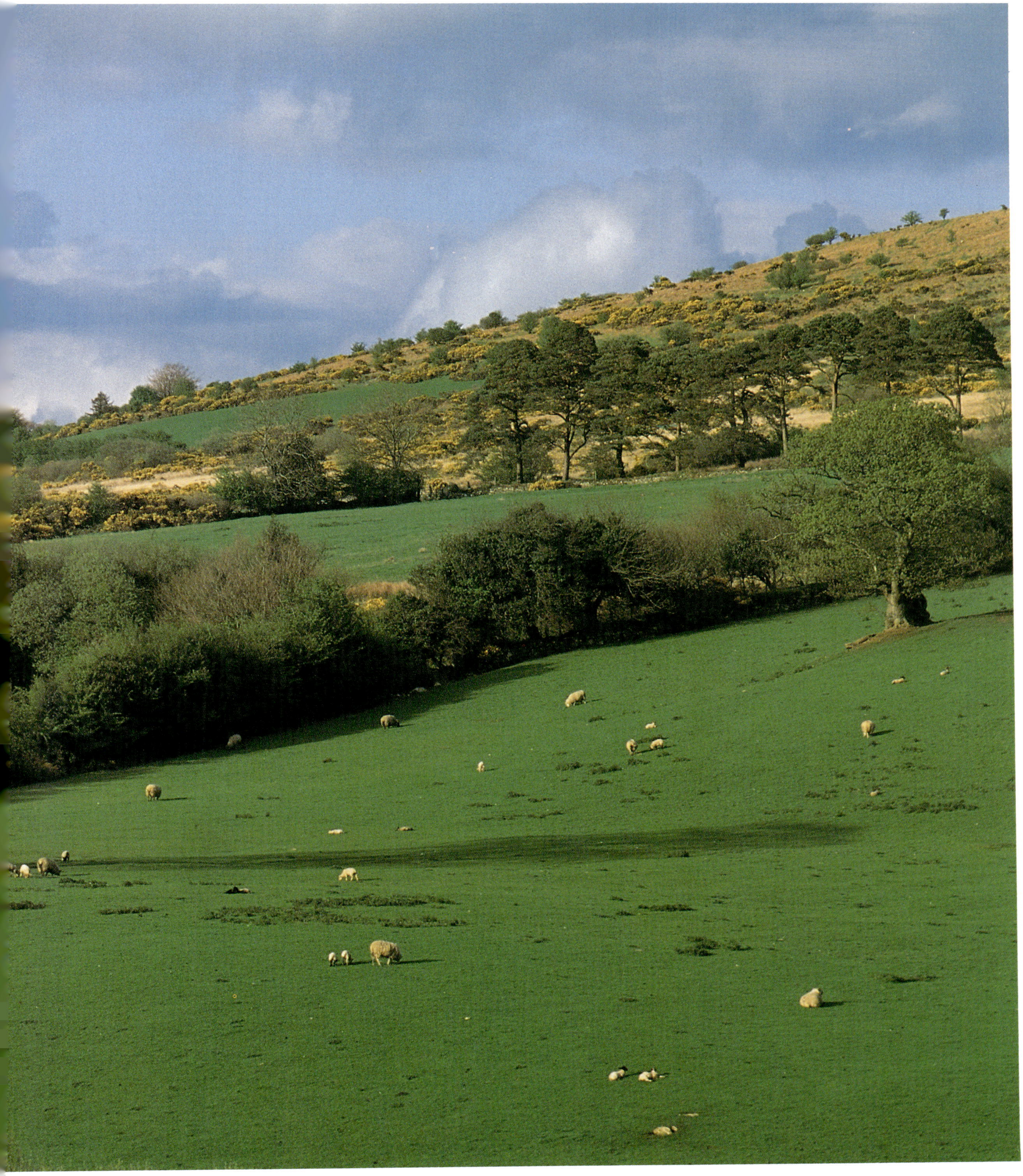

The ruins of Rosserrly Abbey are in the middle of a landscape of rivers and meadows, near Galway. This monastery was founded in 1351.

Pages 8 and 9: This picture shows how Ireland deserves its reputation as the "Emerald Isle": Sheep grazing on the slopes of the Wicklow mountains.

The extraordinary island

Sláinte

At some time or another, the visitor asks himself what he has really seen of Ireland. There is always the nagging fear that an Irishman will speak to the visitor on the street or in a pub, listen to his vivid impressions and say: "Good heavens, what does he really know about us?"

When we travel, we carry preconceived ideas and images of the places we are visiting. Tourist boards encourage us to think in such clichéd terms, reinforcing the stereotypes. Ireland is a case in point. It sells itself as the Emerald Isle. The glossy brochures are full of majestic mountains, lush river valleys, quaint villages and cottages, grand romantic castles, pubs filled with music and conversation. The country in the brochures is slow-moving, charmingly old-fashioned, a place where the stresses of ordinary life simply fade away. Ireland: the green island in the Atlantic.

Like all clichés it has a basis in truth, but it also exaggerates and distorts the picture. For Ireland is not a fantasy land. It is a country in which the old and the new are thrown together in a fascinating mix. It is modernising at a high speed, while trying to retain the best of the old ways. It has the youngest population in Western Europe, one of the biggest computer software industries in the EU and a brilliant new generation of writers who are renewing one of the island's most enduring traditions. The cities are buzzing with creativity. And yet, in the quieter rural parts, it is still possible to think of this as the land that time forgot. You can sit in a quiet country pub, sipping your Guinness and listening to the ticking of the clock behind the bar and imagine that this is how the world was long ago.

History

Ireland is like a castle, with electric lighting already installed to be sure, but otherwise they are still busily working on restoration, and painters are constantly working on livening up the building with bright colours. Alongside the predominant tones of yellow ochre, brown and silvery grey and through all shades of green, a strong red shines forth here, and a warm blue or a bright yellow there. This grand and impressive landscape, with its shores washed by the Atlantic, idyllic river scenes, wild coastline, green meadows, white houses, grey ruins, is absolutely fascinating. No wonder the island has many friends; but most of those who visit are individualists, mass tourism is little known here.

Ireland is history. It has undergone constant change because for centuries, indeed thousands of years, invaders and conquerors have come and gone. The island has been continuously inhabited for almost 10,000 years. It contains the oldest recorded site of human habitation in Europe, at Mount Sandel, in Co. Derry, which archaeologists have dated to almost 6000 B.C. The great passage grave at Newgrange, Co. Meath — one of the outstanding achievements of prehistoric Europe — was constructed around 2500

The Rock of Cashel, in a 19th century engraving. The largely visible granite outcrop was the site of an early Celtic royal seat, and in the middle ages it was an ecclesiastical centre.

B.C., at about the same time as the great pyramids of Egypt. All this long predated the Celts, who did not begin to settle in Ireland until as late as about 250 B.C. But, when they did arrive, they swept aside all the pre-existing peoples and completely dominated the island.

Recorded history really begins where Patrick, the first Bishop of Ireland, converted the Celts to Christianity. The new religion established itself with astonishing speed and was soon uniformly spread through the entire island. The early Christian period, from about 450 to 800 A.D., is still thought of as Ireland's golden age. The island was not just the centre of learning but also of a great missionary endeavour.

Ireland was in religious terms the focal point of Europe, with Irish monks doing missionary work on the continent (St. Gallen is an Irish foundation!). They may also have discovered Greenland and America. Their monastery cells produced such famous manuscripts as the "Book of Kells" and the "Book of Durrow", which today can be admired in the library of Trinity College, Dublin. Today countless Irishmen are still called Patrick, with Paddy as a diminutive and a nickname; a *Paddy joke* is an Irish joke.

Finally, in the eighth century, Celtic and early Christian Ireland was overcome by the marauding Vikings. The men from the North built thick walls around their settlements. The towns of Dublin, Wicklow, Limerick, Cork, Wexford and Arklow are among the settlements they founded. Three hundred years later, the Vikings were finally contained by the Irish king, Brian Boru. Under this chieftain, who has entered the annals of Irish history as an immortal hero, the beginnings of political unity in the country were established. But it was a false dawn. There had never been political unity in Gaelic Ireland under a single dominant king. Brian succeeded briefly, but, after his death in 1014, the old pattern resumed. The various kingdoms, large and small, fought each other incessantly. There was nothing peculiar about this. Classical Greece was no different to Gaelic Ireland in having a series of independent territories which fought each other for influence, but all of whom feared the emergence of a single all-powerful central government which would erode their local independence.

Among other buildings, there is a thirteenth century cathedral on the Rock of Cashel. It is a typical example of Gothic architecture. Although the roof is missing, it conveys something of the stateliness of a medieval diocesan church.

A detail from the innumerable examples of masonry work which are both in the cathedral and in Cormac's Chapel, a gem of Irish tenth century architecture, on the rock of Cashel.

The British Conservative Party leader, Bonar Law, speaking in 1912 to demonstrators against Irish Home Rule.

Scenes from the Irish war of independence. An armoured police vehicle controlling a demonstration march in Sackville Street, Dublin.

Eamon de Valera, legendary leader of the Irish republican movement, and later first President of the Irish Republic, at a protest meeting in Dublin, in the 1920s.

In 1169, the first Anglo-Norman settlers arrived. The Normans had conquered England in 1066. Now they quickly established themselves in Ireland, sustained by their superiority in arms. They captured the towns and fortified them to a degree never before seen in Ireland. They settled much of the best land. Their king, Henry II of England, followed in 1172 in order to stop the establishment of an independent Norman kingdom in Ireland. He promptly declared himself Lord of Ireland.

The Normans were still outnumbered by the Gaels. Gradually, force of numbers told. Some Normans became Gaelicised; others inter-married; in many parts Gaelic chieftains recovered lost lands. In general, both groups worked out a *modus vivendi* for most of the Middle Ages, although the principal Norman families - the Butlers and the FitzGeralds - were dominant.

Then came the Reformation. Tudor England turned Protestant and developed a highly centralised state. Ireland remained Catholic, in defiance of the general European rule which stated that a people must follow their king in matters of religion. Gaels and Normans alike clung to the old faith. England now attempted a new conquest of the island, the better to establish its authority both in church and state. Under Queen Elizabeth, the Nine Years' War (1592-1601) brought the destruction of Ulster, the most Gaelic part of medieval Ireland. The old Gaelic aristocracy was expropriated and a new class of English and Scots "planters" was settled on the land. These people were the antecedents of today's Northern Ireland Protestants.

Other wars followed. In the 1640s, Oliver Cromwell dispossessed all Catholic landowners in the provinces of Leinster and Munster, handing over their lands to new English Protestant settlers. The Catholics - whether of Norman or Gaelic stock now mattered less and less - tried unsuccessfully to restore their fortunes and were finally defeated in 1691. There followed the century of the Protestant Peace, in which the rule of

In Cork's covered markets, there is a wide choice of vegetables, dairy produce, meat, and of course fresh sea food or smoked salmon.

the colonial ascendancy was unchallenged. Much of its benign legacy, especially in architecture, is still there to be seen.

Irish nationalism developed from the 1790s onwards. It was mainly, although not exclusively, Catholic. The mainstream nationalist tradition was political, but a minority segment believed in violence. For most of the nineteenth century the political tradition was strongest, first under Daniel O'Connell then under Charles Stewart Parnell in the second. At the mid-century, a devastating Famine killed a million people and caused another million to emigrate - the start of the modern Irish Diaspora.

Finally, in 1916, the violent tradition in Irish nationalism had its apotheosis. A Rising in Dublin against the British rule set in train a series of events that resulted in independence for most of Ireland in 1922. But the Protestants of Ulster, a local majority descended from the seventeenth-century settlers, rejected independence. Northern Ireland remained within the UK. However, it did not adhere to normal British standards and for almost fifty years treated its Catholic minority as second-class citizens. The present Northern Ireland troubles stem from the Catholic efforts to achieve equality of citizenship, although the IRA - heirs to the tradition of Irish nationalist violence - have effectively declared war on the very nature of the state itself.

The faces of Ireland

The Irish are thought of as a jolly, friendly, and peace-loving people. They can, however, be as boisterous and loud as any other people. They have a disarming warmth and

People in Ireland: Not all of them fit the stereotype of red hair and freckles.

sincerity, and their ever-present laughter is as honest as anywhere else in Europe. Yet behind their joviality lurks a mysterious sadness, which finds expression in the country's melancholy songs and magnificent literature.

Ireland is counted amongst Europe's oldest indigenous cultures. Despite the turbulence of its history, the island's relative isolation has enabled it to retain a large number of its traditional ways. The more remote western parts have retained most. It was here that the Irish language - the old Gaelic tongue - survived longest and may still be heard in certain areas. Ireland's exceptional contribution to world literature has been greatly enhanced by the oral tradition of storytelling, cultivating a passion for words and their correct use in narrative or dramatic context. Traditional music is now experiencing a glorious revival. Ireland is one of the few countries in Europe whose folk music was almost untouched by court or classical music.

This small island has become a favoured holiday destination for Americans and Europeans. The Irish Tourist Board, which might as well be called The Welcome Department, has played a decisive role in this. Tourism makes one of the most important contributions to the economy of a country with almost no industrially usable raw materials. The "natural raw material" is the landscape in its variety, with the moors, heathland, mountains, lakes, seashores, cliffs and largely unspoilt nature. Most buildings are low-rise, with few skyscrapers even in the cities, while the superb coastline is for the most part unspoiled. Nowhere on the island is the sea ever more than 100 kilometres away. Most visitors come from America, England, France and Germany. Ireland has also been successful in attracting foreign industries. The financial incentives and the tax relief which the government has granted have been decisive factors, as has been the availability of a cheap labour force, and also, but unfortunately, the low expenditure on environmental matters. Guinness Stout, Irish Whiskey and tweed from Donegal are trade names known worldwide, as is also Waterford crystal and much more.

The traveller who has come to look and enjoy must establish priorities, and learn the art of what to leave out. The island offers so much variety, as only a land so pampered by its climate can; the snow-covered tops of the Twelve Bens shine forth in the April sunshine, while in nearby Clifden bay you can get an early Spring sun-tan by the sea. Then again, you can ride through the high moors of Mayo, without meeting a soul all day, or play at Robinson Crusoe on the coasts of Donegal, or perhaps feel like a feudal prince on Garinish Island, in its gardens with their oriental atmosphere. Time and again the visitor is fascinated by the superabundance of light, which gives the sea a fresh turquoise colour and bathes the land in a radiant, overwhelming brilliance, which in its crystalline transparency creates a Mediterranean feel.

The roads are another experience. For most European or American visitors, used to motorways and inter-state highways, they seem terribly narrow. However, most main roads in Ireland are now improving rapidly. There are as yet few motorways, but generally the principal trunk routes are adequate for the amount of traffic that they have to bear. Most, though not all, of the really narrow stretches of main road have now been widened or bypassed. In general, driving in Ireland is a pleasant experience which benefits - like so much else here - from the low population density.

The secondary roads are another matter altogether. They <u>can</u> be good, but don't depend upon it! Some are very narrow, some are badly potholed, and yet. . . yet they can be part of the charm of the country. No one who has driven on the little road that snakes around Slea Head in Co. Kerry would ever wish to see a corniche built here - even if such things were possible.

For generations Ireland's most important export has been its people. Even today about 500 people, mostly young, leave their homeland every week. Traditionally, Irish people took few skills abroad. Happily, this is not now always the case. Some young Irish emigrants are educated to a very high level and take full advantage of the free movement of labour within the European Union.

For many Irish, especially men, emigration is a romantic myth, and a challenge. "For many it's a test of courage", said a spokeswoman for the "Youth Emigration Action Group" in Dublin, founded in 1985. "It's a disgrace for our country, that thousands of the most able and most intelligent people still have to emigrate. The government must act to help." But it faces the same problem as other Western governments - youth unemployment. Service with powerful paymasters has a long history: the Irish were on Columbus' caravels, took part in the Crusades, helped the English, the Dutch and the Spaniards to conquer their colonies, laid railway lines right across America, and ruined their health in the mines.

Today the United States has about 44 million citizens of Irish origin, the Irish Americans are Ireland's greatest sponsors, and they are very keen to revisit the land of their forefathers.

In June 1984 the village of Ballyporeen, with its 300 souls, was the stage of a great spectacle: US President Ronald Reagan came on a visit. His father was the son of a farmer, John Reagan, who had emigrated to the United States in 1854, and supposed to have been a devout catholic - and well known for his drinking. He had left Ireland in the years after the famine. From an Irish farm cottage to the White House in Washington in three generations - a not untypical Irish career. The fact that millions of other Irish have not climbed that rapidly does not worry the migrants. US presidents are the best advertisements for emigrating to the United States though: Andrew Jackson, Richard Nixon and John F. Kennedy were presidents of Irish descent as well.

Many Irish people remember President Kennedy's visit in 1963, as though it were only yesterday, because Kennedy said then: "No nation did more to preserve Christendom and keep Western culture alive in their darkest hours. No nation did more to keep the flame of independence alive in America, indeed in the whole world. And none of the larger nations of the world has given the world more writers and artists of genius."

Continuation page 35

Top: Dublin's brightly coloured doors, striking dabs of colour on otherwise rather grey houses, are among the Irish capital's well known "trade marks".

Double spread overleaf: View of the River Liffey in Dublin. On the right, in the foreground, five-lane traffic flowing over O'Connell Bridge. The Liffey Bridge and Grattan Bridge are visible in the background.

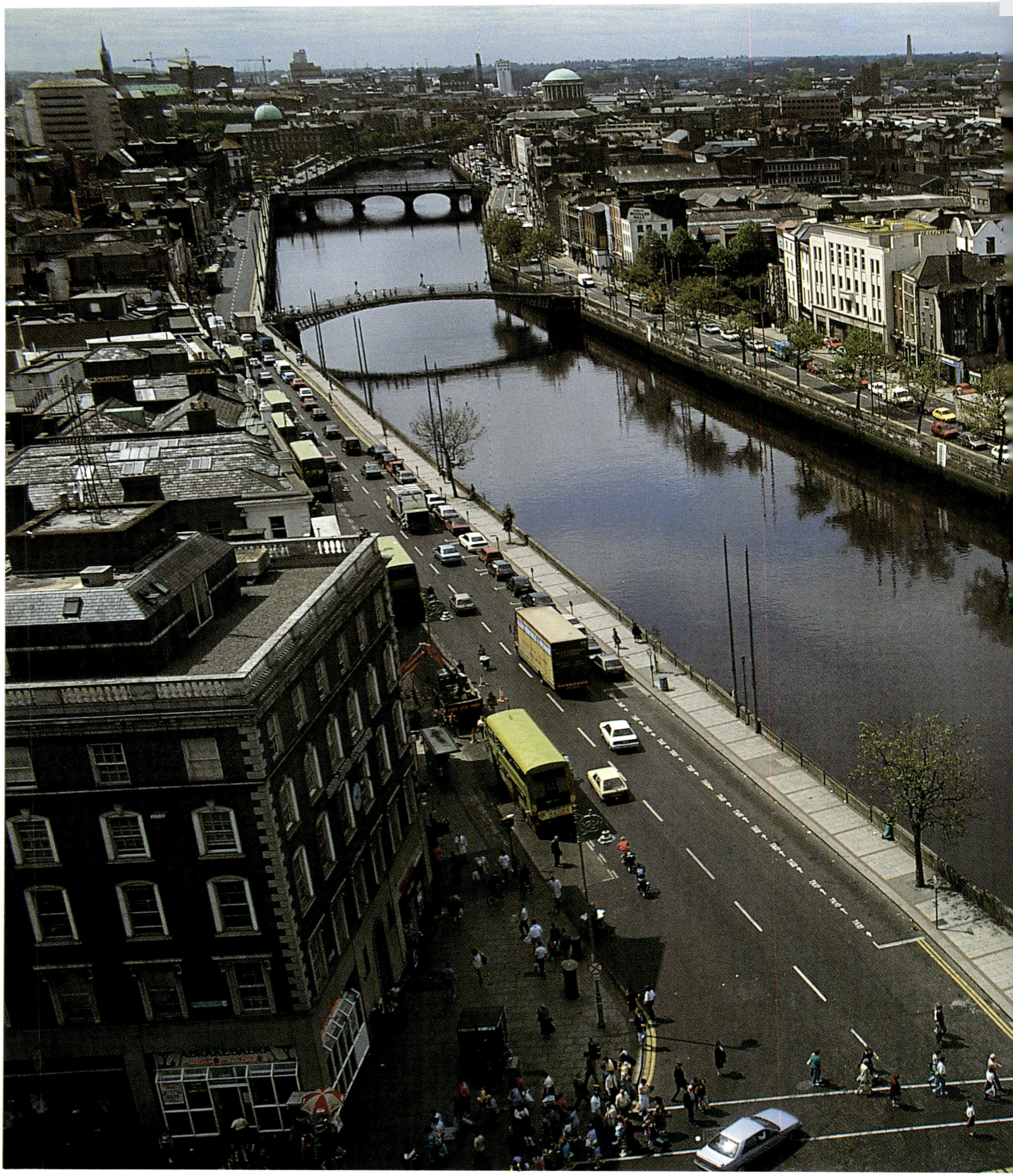

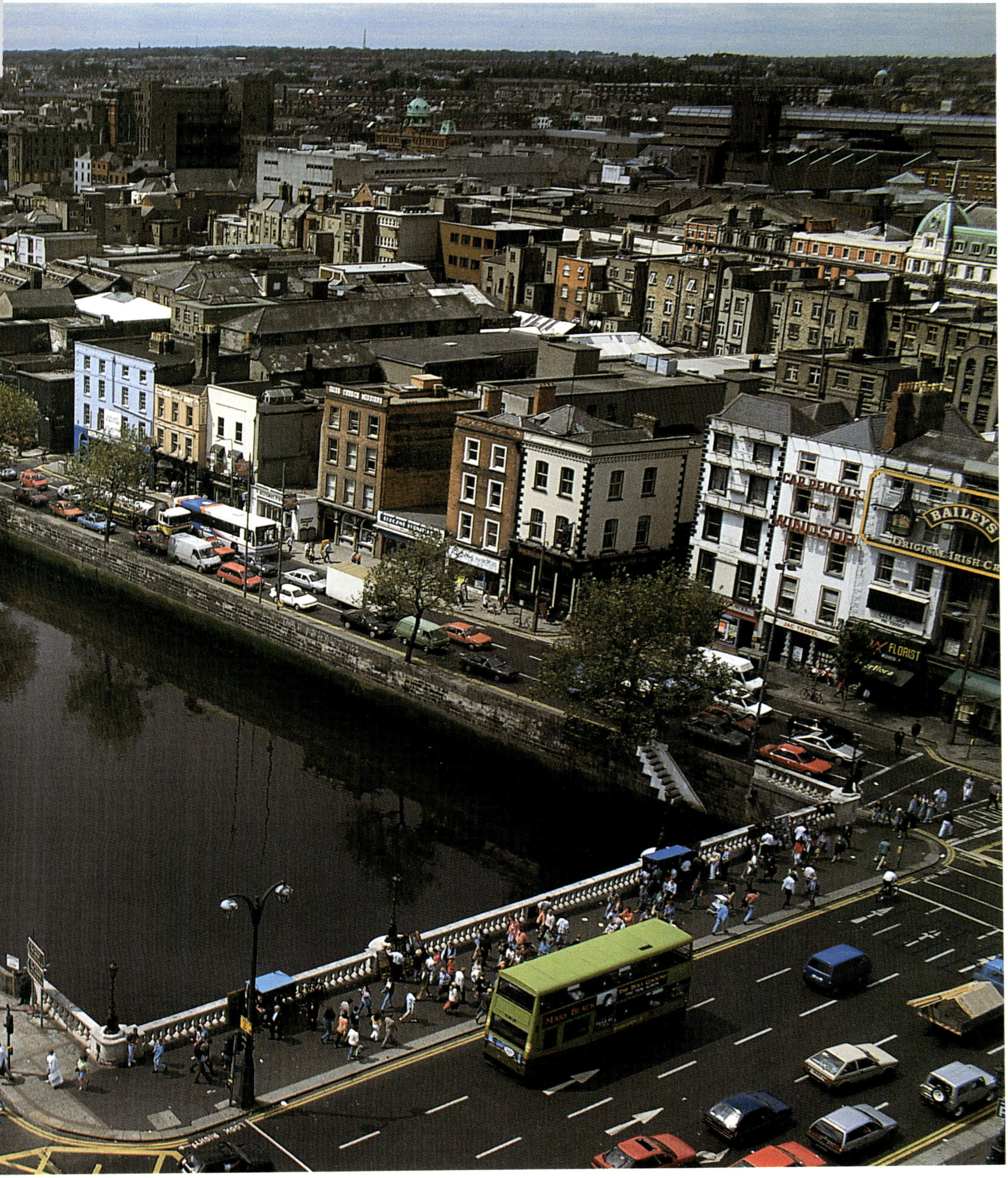
CAR RENTALS
WINDSOR
BAILEYS
FLORIST

Trinity College, Dublin's 16th century university, which counts Jonathan Swift, Oscar Wilde and Samuel Beckett among its past students.

Liffey Bridge, built in 1816, is a feat of British engineering from the early part of the "new iron age". Because of the toll which those passing over it formerly had to pay, this footbridge is popularly known as "Halfpenny Bridge".

A mobile trader sets out his stall in central Dublin.

Double spread overleaf: A look into the library of Trinity College: the 60-metre Long Room houses the finest early Christian manuscripts in Ireland.

EX DONO
CC

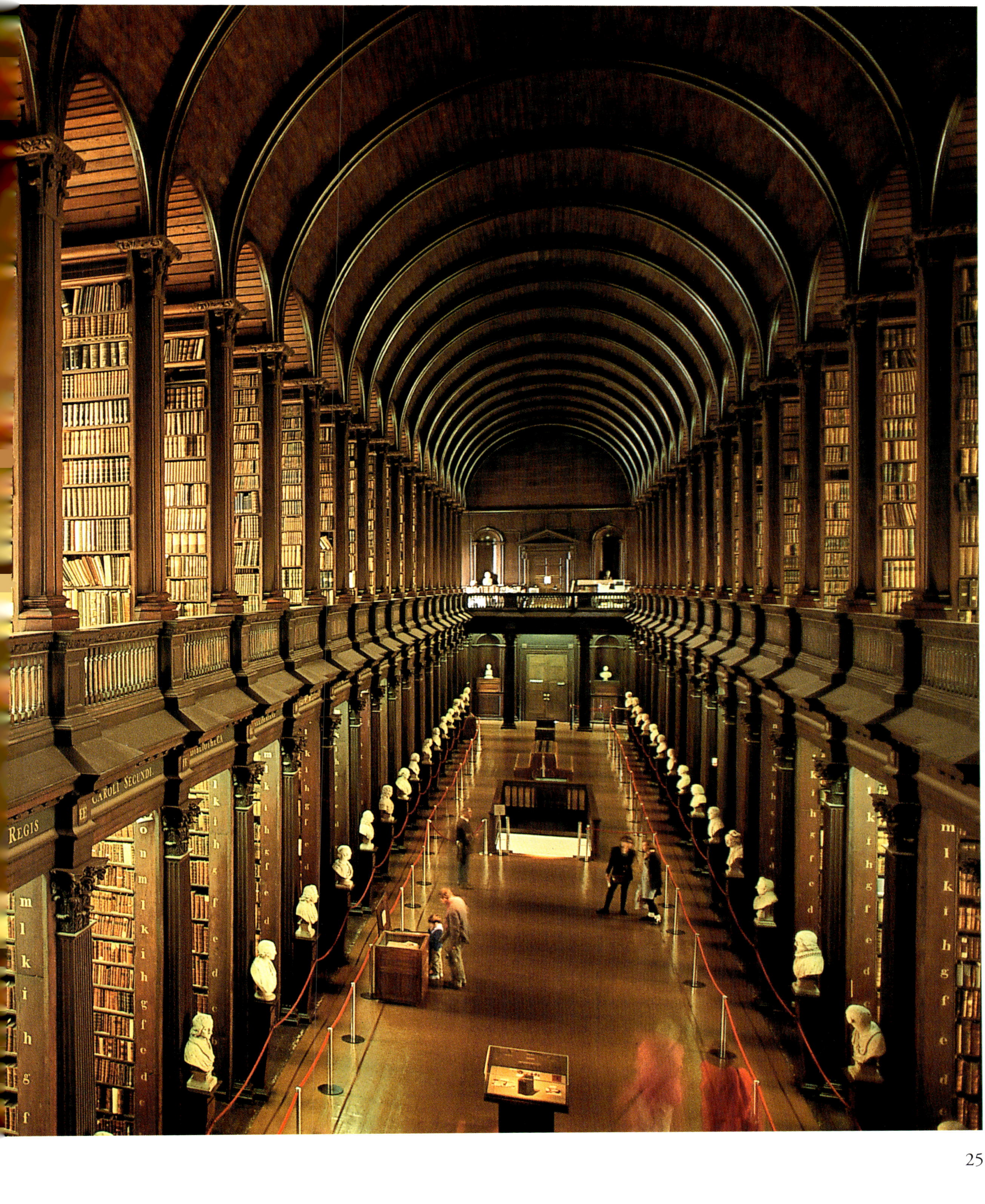
REGIS
ET
CAROLI SECUNDI

Musicians are a common sight on Dublin's streets. They mostly play traditional folk music, enjoyed by residents and tourists alike.

A much-favoured place for Dubliners to buy their fruit and vegetables is the open-air market in Moore Street.

This young man, at the foot of the James Joyce statue, is printing private newspapers to order.

Not much is left of the Monasterboice monastery on the East coast of Ireland, apart from the round tower. It was burnt out in 1097. In front of the tower is the most beautiful of Ireland's high crosses; this cross, almost six metres tall, is decorated with biblical scenes.

Memento mori: a graveyard near Coolaney.

Weathered gravestones in the old churchyard of Glendalough, a monastery town founded by St. Kevin

Ireland is one of the bastions of golf; caressed by a great soft breeze from the Irish sea, golfing must be a very special pleasure amidst the splendid scenery in Wicklow.

In between the picturesque hills of the Wicklow Mountains, there are almost untouched valleys with high moors and heathlands, green meadows, and woods with oak trees. Political refugees, criminals, and outlaws found a hiding place here well into the eighteenth century. Small settlements, like this one near Tullow, are typical of Dublin's "local mountains", in which the inhabitants of the Irish capital more than anyone else, find recreation.

The Irish Sea beats against the rocky coastline at Baily, just a few miles away from Dublin. Baily lighthouse was built in 1814 on the site of an old stone fort.

Double spread overleaf: Newcastle, County Wicklow. A church with its half decayed graveyard, produces a dramatic effect in the light produced by a gathering storm.

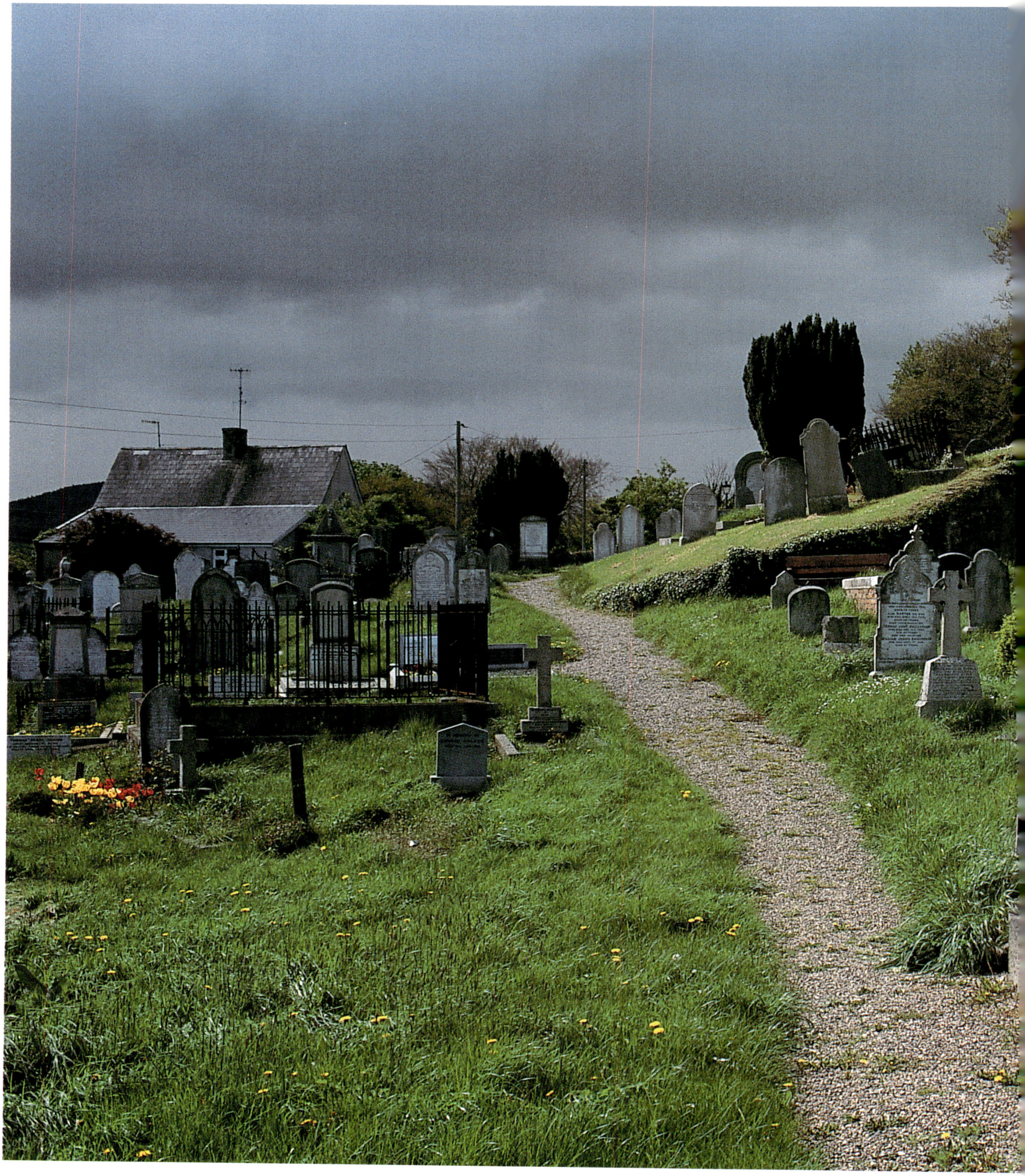

33

The monastery town of Glendalough, founded in the 6th century, in the Wicklow Mountains, is one of Ireland's most important places of pilgrimage. Seen here is St. Kevin's church, built from hard mica schist, with its steep roof and round clock tower.

Pubs - An Irish Institution

Generally speaking, pubs are dark places, pervaded by rather dim light. The outside world stays on the other side of the door, though it provides the topics of conversation, without which life would be impossible here. Characteristics of the bar itself are not just the shiny chrome taps, but the collection boxes as well, which are used to collect for both God and the world: "Please help our foreign mission", "Please support the handicapped", "Help for the Third World", "Life Boats need your help", "Saint Camillus, patron of the sick and dying", and so on. And in pubs like Quinlan's of Tralee, where the creaking floorboards behind the counter have sawdust spread over them, or Neary's of Chatham Street, Dublin, with its over-ornate Victorian pomp - a public house like this embodies Irish life in its more friendly and attractive moments.

The Irish national drink, the "wine of the Irish", is the dark stout with the creamy head, of which about two million pints a day find their way into about ten and a half thousand bars, and down into thirsty throats. As far back as 1815, Wellington's cavalry officers drank this dark liquid; today worldwide, about 9 million glasses of it are emptied every day - partly to the benefit of this island in the Atlantic. All the ingredients for this beer are home produced: malt, yeast, hops, barley and of course, Irish water. The Guinness brewery, founded in 1759, employs about 5,000 people and is Ireland's largest private company. It says a lot about Ireland that the plans for "Dublin, European Cultural Centre, 1991" were presented to the international press in the brewery. The country exploits its citizens' thirst, the tax on beer being the highest in the EU. According to an *Irish Times* survey, people are hoping among other things for a reduction in beer tax from a united Europe. Although the days are gone when men and women had separate compartments, in some pubs you still find the *snug* - closed off corners with a door which can only be opened from the inside - from the days when women were not admitted to the pub and drinking in public was still a man's business. Vestiges of these old distinctions remain in the division of most pubs into two sections, bar and lounge. The bar is cheaper, more male orientated and less well appointed. Some bars remain defiantly men only in fact, if not in theory. There is also a class element in all this. The bar is more working-class than the lounge, and most middle-class men prefer to patronise the lounge. In general, the bar is more likely to be more old-fashioned, more raucous and more smokey than the lounge.

Some of Ireland's finest pubs do not observe the distinction at all, however. A single room is all there is. In Dublin, pubs as famous as Ryan's of Parkgate Street, Doheny & Nesbitt's, the Old Stand and The Long Hall are of this kind: you just go inside and it is the same for everybody. This is also true of many smaller country pubs.

A good pub is a boon and a blessing. It is a social centre, a place to relax, somewhere to meet friends, a focus for the neighbourhood. The two main occupations are drinking and talking, until the barman calls last drinks at 11.30 p.m. and the unsolved problems of the world have to be postponed until tomorrow.

Traditional and Modern

Ireland has more to offer than history and libraries full of folios, in which that history is recorded. Nor does it consist just of monuments from the stone age, castle ruins, walls of old forts and round towers, bearing silent witness in the landscape to a long cultural tradition. There is a lot about Ireland which is lively, too. The true nature of this island can best be experienced if you approach it quite irreverently - without constantly thinking about how time and men have taken their toll. This land and its barely five million inhabitants is never short of surprises.

The Irish have music in their blood. Traditional music can be heard especially in folk clubs and pubs, played on typical instruments.

Pubs are not the exclusive domain of men any more. Young and old meet here, of either sex. A baby at the bar is nothing unusual.

WHISKEY AND BLACK BEER

This country knows three symbols; The harp, shamrock, and black beer. When the brewer Arthur Guinness founded his brewery in 1759, with the help of the Anglican archbishop of Cashel, beer as a drink was virtually unknown to the Irish. People drank whiskey, gin, and poteen. The last of these was, and is, a clear, pale concoction from illegal stills with only one outstanding characteristic - you get drunk on it quickly. Guinness brewed this new, black, porter beer so as to stand out from the other breweries, and was immediately successful. In 1790 the beer was already being sold in London pubs, and was first sold in continental Europe in 1815. In Ireland, people called it the *parish priest*, as a well-tapped black beer with the white creamy head on it presumably reminded the Irish faithful of a priest's cassock. The recipe for this beer which is drunk worldwide is made up of hops, yeast, water and barley; one part of the barley is malted, and the other part is roasted; that is how the stout gets its dark colour. All the ingredients come from Ireland. And it is obvious to the Irish that no Guinness tastes as good as the one in your own pub, and there are thousands of them on the island, in which more than two thirds of the drinks poured are the black beer. This bitter beer has been making its victorious way round the world for a long time now, It is poured out in 140 countries, and made the Anglo-Irish Guinness family rich.

Whiskey was not invented by the Scots, but by the Irish, and here they spell it with an "e". The first licence was granted to the whiskey distillery in Bushmills, in 1608, and since then the Irish have been brewing a pleasant-tasting, mild whiskey from barley. Irish Whiskey, or "water of life" (in Gaelic "Uisge beatha") has been made at least since the twelfth century, when King Henry II's invading soldiers were paid in whiskey. There were hundreds of small, privately-owned distilleries in Ireland in the eighteenth and nineteenth centuries. It was a risky business, with a high failure rate. Today, there is just one: Irish Distillers, which maintains a major distillery in Midleton, Co. Cork and a smaller - but very historic - one in Bushmills, Co. Antrim. Irish Whiskey gets its classic malt taste from malted barley, which is dried out in closed cauldrons. The whiskey may only be sold after at least five year's storage, which must be in wooden barrels. In the Irish Whiskey Corner, in Bow Street, Dublin, the history of the drink is abundantly documented, and the Old Distillery in Midletown, Co. Cork also tells the story of the "Irish Gold".

Supposedly it was in a pub in the village of Foynes, Co. Limerick, that Irish coffee was invented in the fifties, that hot drink - with any luck - made from strong black coffee, sugar, whiskey and whipped cream, which should be drunk without stirring it. The Irish, however, prefer to drink their whiskey neat or with a little water.

Irish pubs are not just places where you can get a drink; they are meeting places of a quite special kind.

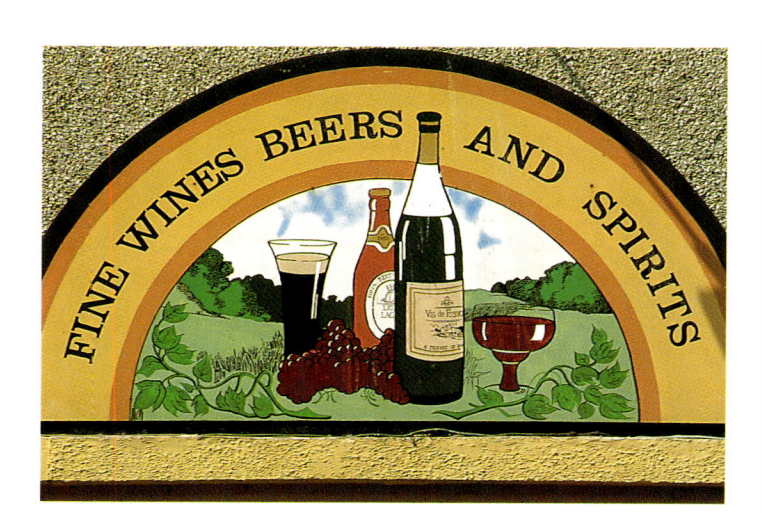

Also very much part of the place are the goats, wild donkeys and sheep. The latter, with their brightly coloured identification spots, are everywhere - on the high moors of Mayo, the dunes of Donegal, and around the loughs of Connemara; they run straight across the minor roads, which are narrow enough anyway, and can only be moved aside with patience. The sheep in particular are quite unpredictable: one of them might suddenly change its mind, and run back again. They can even negotiate quite effortlessly the stone walls which are built all over the country, in their tireless search for food.

Stone walls. All over Ireland, but especially in the western counties, these are to be found everywhere. They are used as boundary markers and as windbreaks. The art of constructing a dry-stone wall - that is, one where the stones rest naturally one upon the other with no mortar or cement to bind them together - is a very ancient skill and one, moreover, which is by no means unique to Ireland. Such stone walls may be found in many remote and upland places in Scotland or the North of England - the Yorkshire Dales, for example. But, for sheer profusion, there are few places where they can be found more readily than in the West of Ireland. Co. Galway has a particularly fine network of dry-stone walls and, when one ventures to the Aran Islands, just off the coast in Galway Bay, one meets a veritable riot of stone. Here, the incessant Atlantic winds have stripped

Brightly coloured signs invite you in for a drink. Pubs occupy a central position in Irish life;

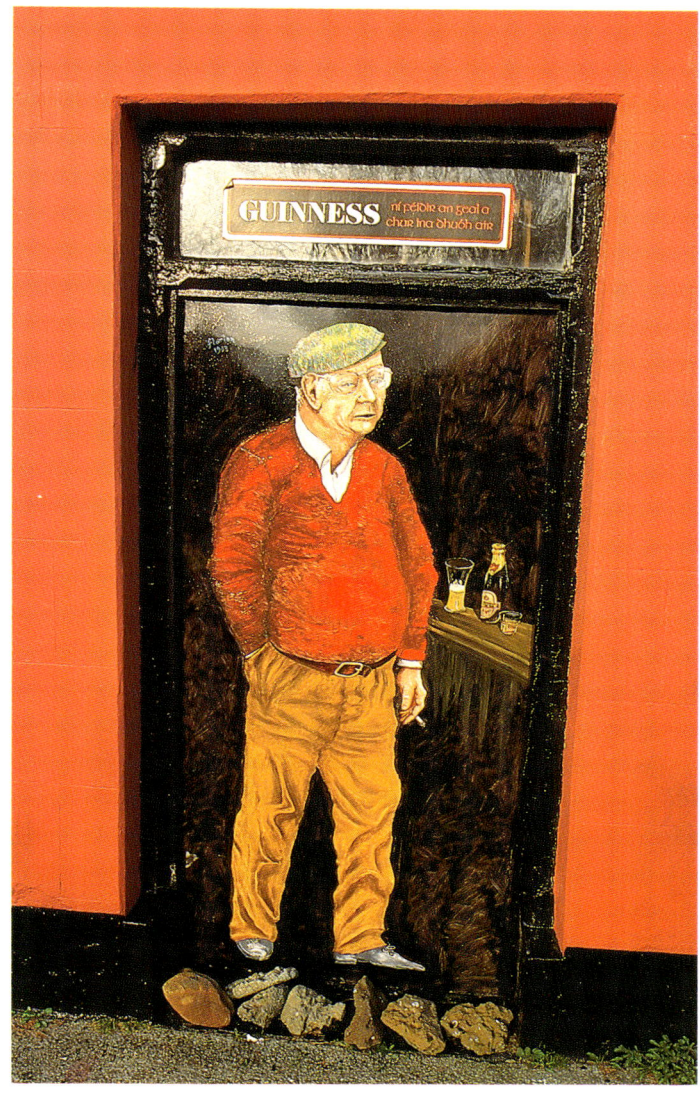

in smaller places a general store and pub are often run together.

the thin topsoil away, exposing the stone underneath, so that the very ground itself seems like a table of stone. And on all sides the walls rise in a dizzying profusion to create a manmade landscape unlike anything anywhere in the world. It is bizarre and strange and very beautiful.

The Irish have a special relationship with stones. Their country is rich in stone artefacts. Among them are about 80 round towers, 30,000 circular walls in stone, dozens of monastery and church ruins, 120 high crosses with Christian motifs. The most beautiful of these is near Monasterboice. The most impressive of the Neolithic tombs is near Newgrange. In the burial chamber, which can be reached through a narrow passage, on the shortest day of the year, that is the winter solstice, the sun falls precisely into the cubiculum. Generations have worked on this passage grave, and for the archaeologists it is still a puzzle how people in about 2500 B.C. were able to stack these erratic blocks, weighing tons, so precisely.

In the country, they talk of "stones with living souls", such as in the Burren, a barren, greyish-white plateau, which glows so strangely, as if the moon were shining on it. No trees, no animals, no people. This area in County Clare is characterised by countless wedge-shaped monumental graves, which people built between 4000 and 2600 B.C., though their origin still lies in prehistoric shadow. A megalith grave visible from far away

Far left: Staigue Fort: this stone fortress, with its circular wall 30 metres in diameter, dates from the iron age. The inside of the walls can be reached over a narrow gangway, and from there a system of stairways leads to the prehistoric buildings.

Left: This shepherd near Leenane still carries a shillelagh, the stick made from blackthorn wood, and used both as a walking stick and as a weapon.

is the Poulnabrone Dolmen, with its colossal cover stone resting across its bearing stones, each weighing tons.

We should not forget two tiny islands in the extreme south west of Ireland, the Skelligs. Only birds can land on the smaller one, Little Skellig, whereas on the larger one people can as well. The bigger island, known as Skellig Michael, was the most dramatic and inaccessible of all the ancient Irish monastic sites. It is an enormous pyramid of rock, visible from fifty kilometres distance along the coast, lashed by the full force of the Atlantic tides and gales. The monastery was probably founded in the early sixth century and appears to have continued in existence for over 600 years. The monastery site lies in a small saddle about 200 metres above sea level, the least exposed part of the entire island. The ruins are still visible and in summer it is possible to travel here from the mainland; there is a small slipway at the foot of the cliff where passengers can disembark before making the long climb up the steps which have been cut into the rockface. The monks who lived, prayed and died here renounced the world of comfort and chose, instead, to cast themselves away in this inhospitable place in order to atone for the sins of mankind.

Some distance north of here, at an inlet called Brandon Cove on the Dingle Peninsula, is the place where, legend has it, St Brendan began the voyage which led him to discover America. St Brendan, usually known in Ireland as "the Navigator", was one of many

Whether they are natural stone formations or dolmens, and Celtic crosses or decayed cottages, stones constantly punctuate the Irish landscape.

41

voyagers of whom it was said that they discovered the North American continent long before Columbus. He lived in the sixth century and the earliest accounts of his voyage date from about 800 A.D. In the early summer of 1976, the explorer Tim Severin made a replica of a sixth-century boat and successfully sailed it to North America, thus proving it would have been possible for St Brendan to have crossed the Atlantic. But whether or not he actually did will always remain a mystery.

Although most visitors come to experience things that are timeless or traditional, it is difficult not to notice that there is a constant dialogue between tradition and modernity in contemporary Ireland. The older certainties of religion and nationality have been eroded by the impact of international consumer culture. This is especially true in the cities, although the impact is felt in the countryside as well. Many Irish people - young people in particular - have grown weary of old ways and want to be as modern and cosmopolitan and fashionable as anyone else. This is especially evident in the impact which Irish music has made on the modern world.

Until the 1970s, there was very little in the way of a pop or rock music industry in Ireland. The previous decade had, however, witnessed an important revival in traditional Irish music. Although this music had always had a place in the lives of ordinary people, it was in danger of being swamped by the radical social changes which the country was beginning to experience. Being traditional and for the most part rooted in the country rather than the towns, it might very well have gone into an irreversible decline. Instead, it experienced a brilliant revival: from ballad groups like the Clancy Brothers and The Dubliners to musicians who have reclaimed and elevated the entire tradition of Irish vernacular music. Of these, the outstanding examples over the past twenty years or so have been The Chieftains. Under the direction of the diminutive Paddy Moloney, The Chieftains have taken the best of the Irish tradition all over the world, to universal and thoroughly deserved critical acclaim.

So the Irish rock revolution, when it came in the seventies, had a hinterland. Ireland was already furnished with a vigorous indigenous popular tradition, and this influenced the way music was played and presented. Bands like Horslips tried to meld rock and traditional Irish, an effort carried on by The Pogues in the eighties. The Chieftains have played with a host of rock stars, including Van Morrison and The Rolling Stones. And all Irish rock musicians are aware of their background in a country that is awash with music and musicians.

Beyond any question the most celebrated Irish band of modern times is U2, surely one of the three or four finest rock bands in the world. In a business littered with early casualties and one-hit wonders, their long reign at the top has been a testimony to the quality of their music and to their sure knowledge of popular taste. Other bands, past and present, which have made a major impact internationally have included The Undertones, The Cranberries and Ash while individual performers like Mary Black and Christy Moore are closer to the folk and ballad tradition.

All in all, popular Irish music of every type is in good shape. It is all part of the fantastic revival of the arts generally in Ireland in the last generation. But it is particularly emblematic of the way the country itself has changed. Old and new, traditional and modern, have happily co-existed and cross-fertilised.

Continuation page 59

Typical cottage near Sneem, Co. Kerry. There are superb fishing grounds in the loughs near this small village.

Double spread overleaf: Ross Beigh juts into Dingle Bay, like a long finger of sand with green dunes and its beautiful sandy inlets.

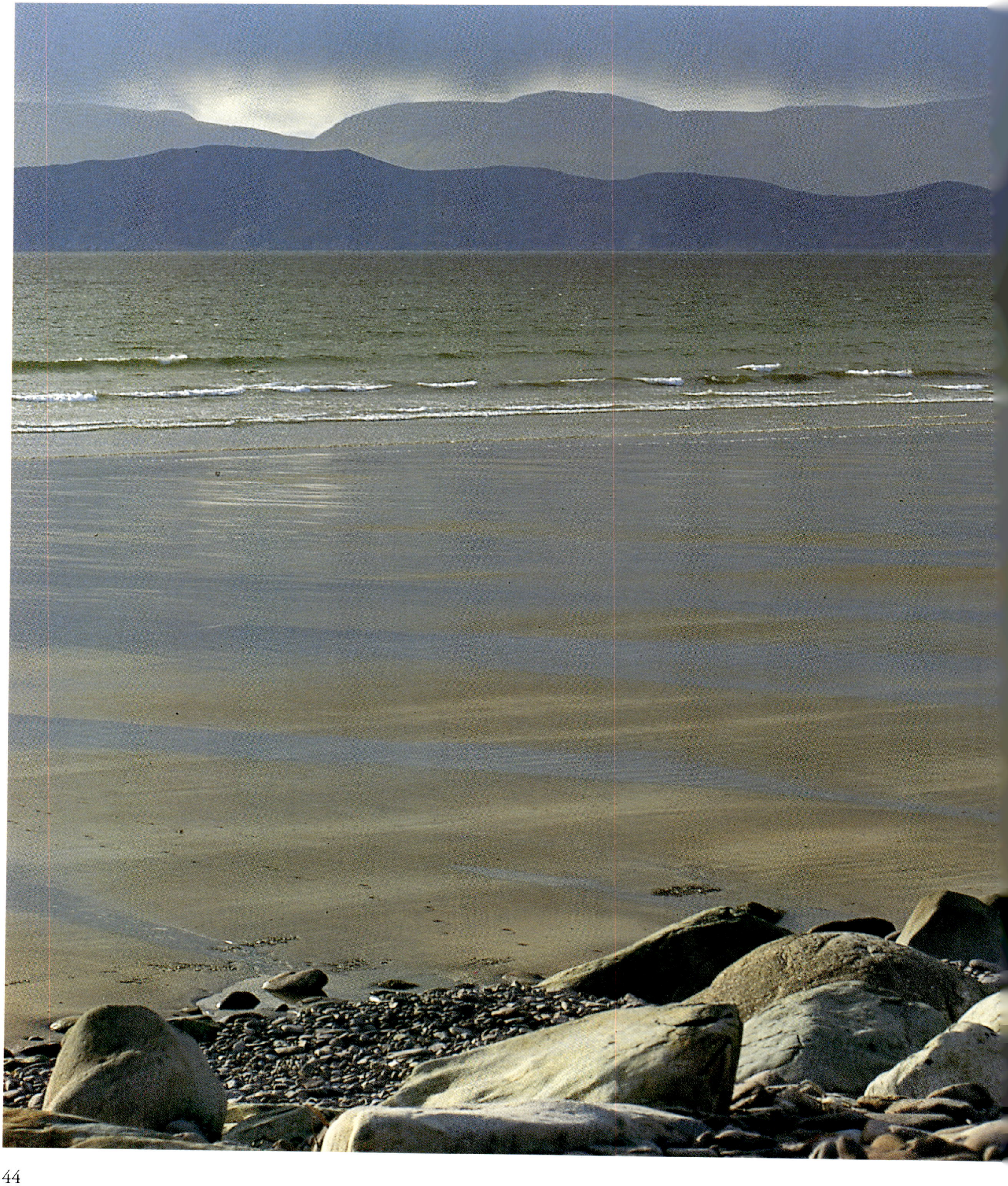

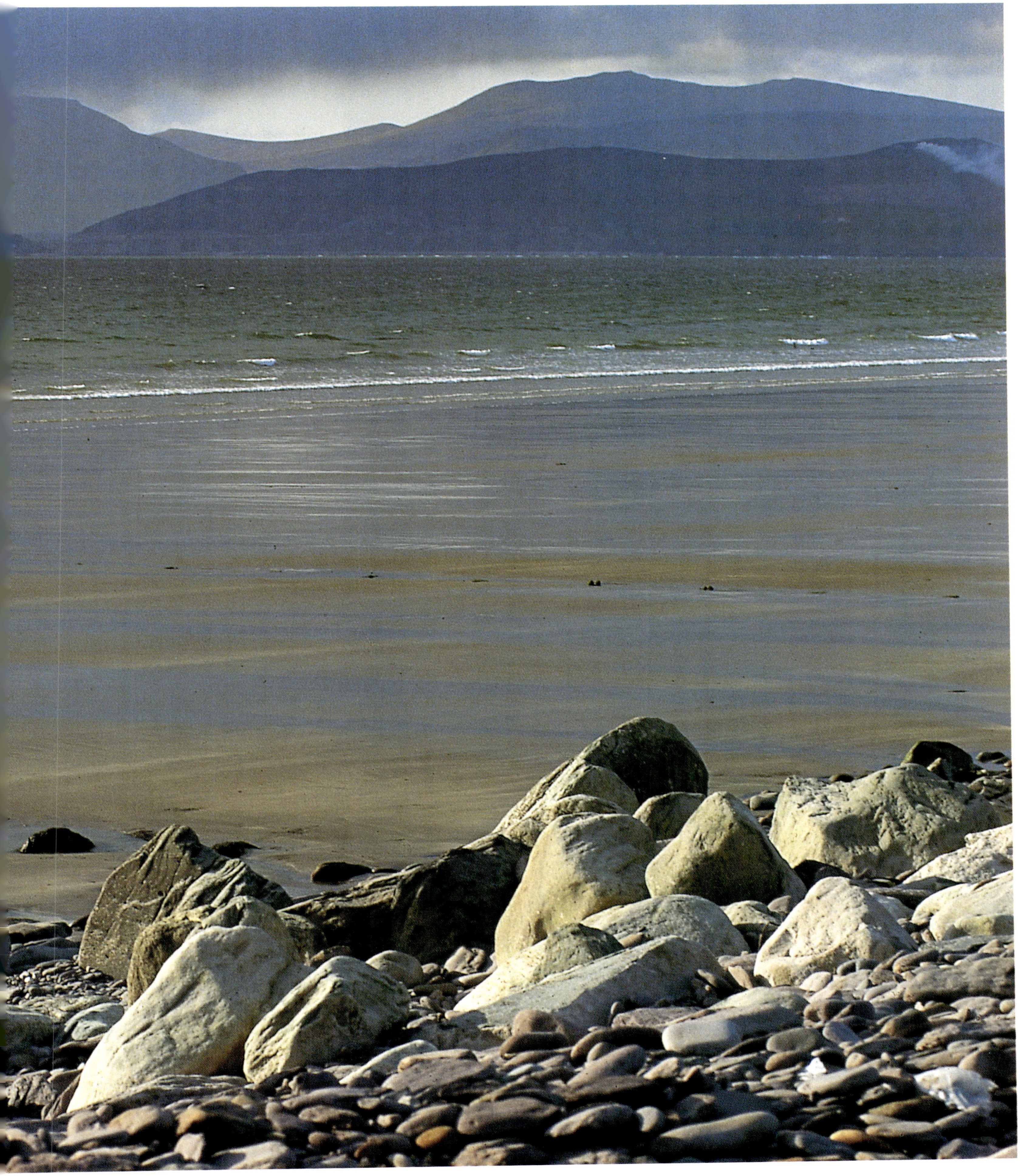

Long, drawn out paths fringed with gorse cut across the whole island, like this one near Castlemaine, Co. Kerry.

Cattle near Sneem: Meat production and dairy farming are traditionally among the most important sources of income for the Irish. Almost 70% of the land - mostly pasture land - is used for agriculture.

A shepherd driving his small herd near Annascaul, on the Dingle peninsula, back to their pen. This picture of an unspoiled world is deceptive, though. Most herds are too small to be economically viable.

Early morning shopping appears to have been done already in Adare, on the west bank of the river Maigue.

The sign of the shamrock at the entrance to this hotel in Kilkenny means that this inn is recommended by the Irish Tourist Board.

A shop in Clonakilty, Co. Cork, being given a bright blue front.

49

A lot of houses in Dingle, the westernmost town in Europe, are brightly coloured, even though some are dilapidated. Dingle used to be a flourishing port with trading links as far away as America. Nowadays the place is more of a small fishing port, but is nevertheless a good starting point for the variety of tourist attractions in the western part of the peninsula of the same name.

Kenmare, with its brightly coloured houses, on the south western tip of Ireland. In this friendly holiday resort ...

... on the Roughty River, there is a lace factory, and in the Poor Clares Convent, one can even watch how this fine handicraft is done.

Dark clouds provide a backdrop for the brightly painted Inns of Killarney

Double spread overleaf: A good 40 miles to the west of Kenmare is Waterville, on a small isthmus between Lough Currane and Ballinskelligs Bay. In Summer the village is a very popular tourist bathing resort.

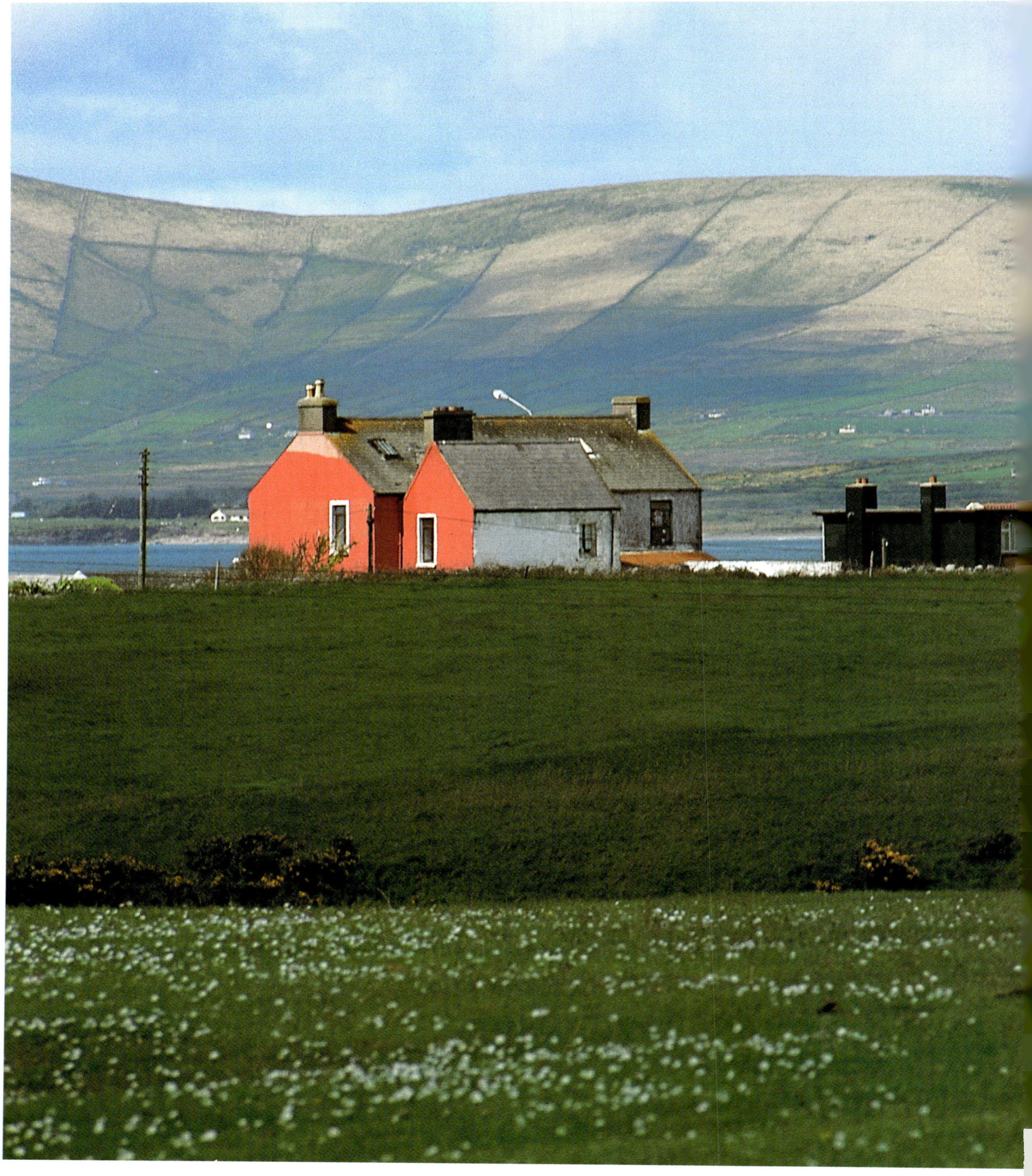

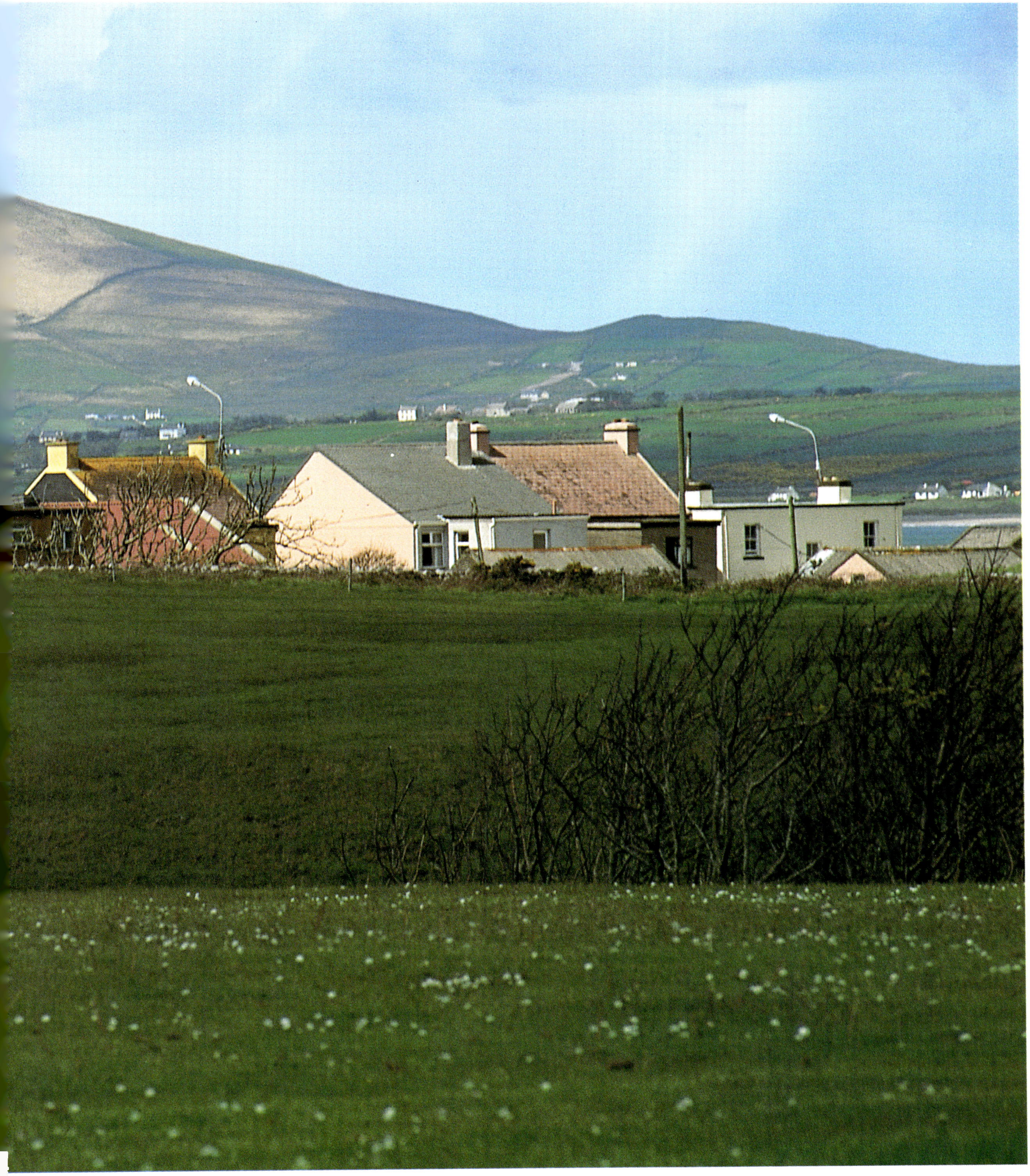

There are seemingly unending breathtaking views on Ireland's west coast. This is at Ross Beigh, in Dingle Bay.

Staigue Fort, near Castlecove, is Ireland's best preserved stone fort. Guesses about what this round masonry structure, about 2500 years old, was used for, range from an "amphitheatre" to a "defensive system against invaders".

Ireland's highest mountains rise up on the Iveragh peninsula. They are only about 3000 feet high, but they are very difficult to climb because of their constantly saturated moorland and the low scrub.

Double spread overleaf: Dingle has a very rugged beauty about it, and is the northernmost of the three picturesque peninsulas in the south west of Ireland.

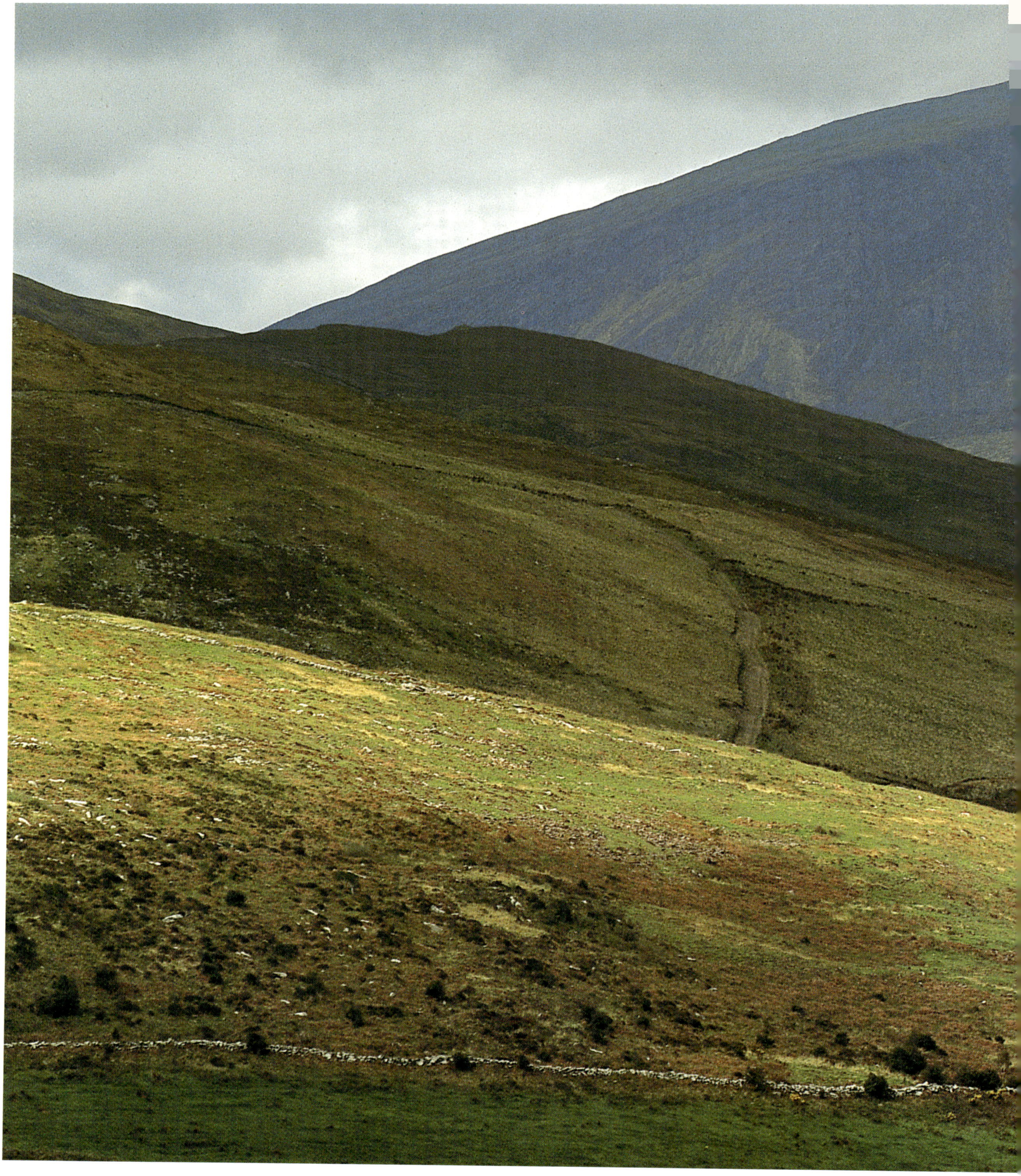

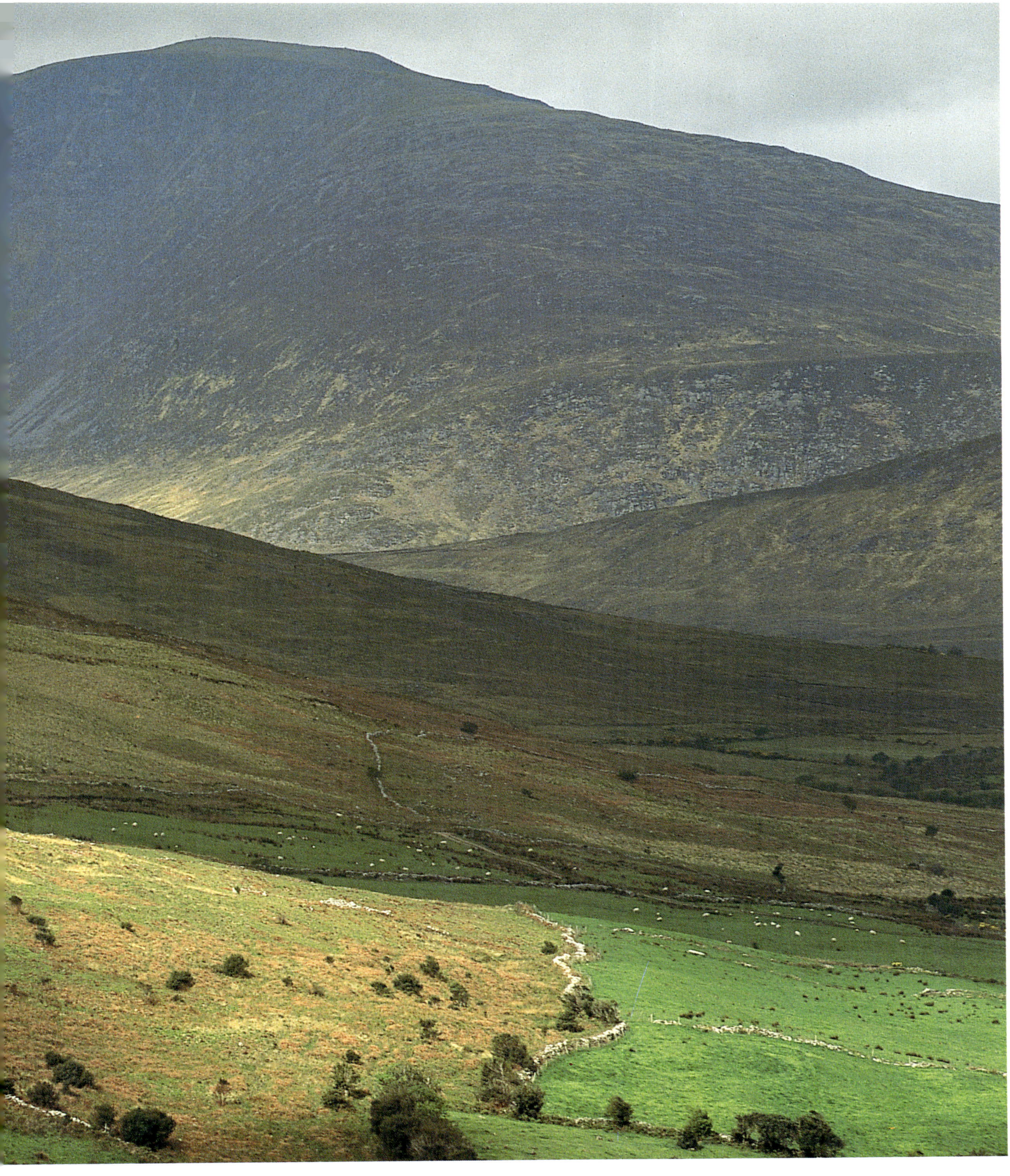

The luxuriant vegetation in Killarney National Park is almost evergreen. The oak trees, wild strawberry plants and bamboos are overgrown with ivy and smothered by huge ferns, and the woodland floor is carpeted with flowers.

"Bed and Breakfast" - An Irish Adventure

Bed and breakfast means one of two things. First, in a hotel it means that you get a room for the night and breakfast the next morning at an inclusive rate. Not all hotels offer it any more - although it used to be the invariable practice. Some of the more expensive hotels offer rates for room only: breakfast, should you wish to eat it, is extra.

Much more to the point is the second meaning of the term. 'Bed and breakfast' means, not an hotel, but a private residence which offers accommodation plus breakfast. Since it is a private house and not an hotel, there is no point in looking for the bar or expecting room service. Having said that, B&B can entail everything from very ordinary, basic accommodation to some really splendid establishments, with extensions to the original house specially built to accommodate guests. The advantages are two-fold. A B&B is always cheaper than an hotel, and almost invariably more friendly. You are, after all, in someone's home and you are treated as a house guest.

Nobody should confuse "B&B" with the continental "Rooms to Let". One is distinguishable from the other not just by its agreeable heartiness, but there is also the sheer excellence of the Irish breakfast, which is something quite special, both in quality and quantity. Here the guest need not get irritated by biscuits which have gone soft, pre-packed portions of butter, orange juice from a carton, tasteless bread rolls, and the accompaniment of muffled background music. In these "B&B" houses, the guest is asked what he would like, the toast comes hot and fresh from the kitchen, the grapefruit juice is freshly pressed, and the tea is a pleasure (the Irish landladies are not so good at making coffee, perhaps it is because of the water), there are bacon and eggs - scrambled, poached or fried - as ordered.

Whether it is in that Georgian mansion in Currarevagh, where the view across Lough Corrib creates a surrealistic dream world atmosphere, or in the white villa on Dooega shore on Achill Island, or the old vicarage in Kinsale, the Ballinghassig farmhouse, or even in Dublin, there is nowhere that is without a "B&B". And to be sure of not being disappointed, you should seek out the houses with the white and green shamrock sign.

So "B&B" from Malin Head in the North, through the Aran Islands in the West, to Baltimore in the South, stands for a fraternity which is quite unique, apart from in England and Scotland. It is characteristic of these small hotels that you can still ask for accommodation late in the evening, and that in the living room for watching TV, there is a peat fire flickering in the hearth, and the rooms have boldly patterned wallpaper in them. And over tea, whether the landlady is a quiet or communicative type, you are treated to a glance into the family chronicles, and the life history of the children is told through the photographs. This kind of friendly treatment is as natural for the landladies as the smell of peat is typical.

More than three million holidaymakers visit the Emerald Isle every year. They all want an experience which has become so rare: nice people, and an unspoiled and uncrowded countryside. Despite all the modernisation, and the bustle in the cities, that is still possible. Sometimes the Irish themselves give the impression that they are a little

Pictures from Ireland as it was at the turn of the century - now a bygone age.

RIGHT AT THE TOP OF THE HIT PARADE: FOLK MUSIC

Well-known Irish music groups such as "the Dubliners", "The Chieftains" or "Clannad", started their careers in the singing pubs. The "Dubliners" and all the other music groups have not only made the music a significant factor in the country's economy, but they have also successfully brought the Irish ballad tradition to a worldwide audience. Here traditional folk music belongs to daily life in a way that it does not do in any other European country. The remoteness of Ireland; the fact that the Irish language survived as a common vernacular in many parts of the country until the middle of the nineteenth century; and the general sense of Irish social solidarity - all have contributed to the survival of the tradition. Nowadays folk music is treasured especially by the more enlightened youth, and should not be confused with pop music. The Irish have traditionally been considered musical and lovers of dancing, and as early as the twelfth century they were described by a chronicler as "incomparably more gifted than any other people". With the decline of Celtic Ireland and conquest by the English (Queen Elizabeth I demanded "All harpists to the gallows!") the old musical traditions were threatened as well. But there was a revival in the eighteenth century, and Irish folklore was taken even to Australia and North America with the emigrants, where they put their own stamp decisively on folk and country music. In the last century several Irish composers created many melodies for the traditional Irish dances, such as jigs, reels and the polka. Although much threatened by the upheavals of the nineteenth century - especially the Famine - the musical tradition survived and flourished. Indeed, it flourished not only in Ireland but among the diaspora as well, especially in America. The real folk revival set in towards the end of the 'fifties.

Irish folk music is considered a fundamental part of earlier European folk music, which had its roots in the agriculture-dominated way of life of the Middle Ages. It was the music which was played and sung at church festivals, on market days, and at weddings, the music which was played during leisure time between the last milking and going to bed. The traditional instruments are the harp, the playing of which was forbidden in 1603, the small Irish bagpipes (*uileann pipes*), the tin-whistle, or penny whistle, a hand drum (the *bódhran*), and the violin, or fiddle. For visitors one of the high points of their visit is when they can listen on the street, at a celebration or in a singing pub, to the often masterly performance of boys and girls, men and women, who draw incredible sounds out of these instruments and are constantly giving new interpretations of already existing melodies, with their own personal variations. The Irish love their music, and they are the only people in the world who have a musical instrument as their national emblem - the harp.

The success which folk music enjoys not only in Ireland speaks for itself, and a new generation is putting new life into traditional Irish ballads and rebel songs, even mixing them with elements of contemporary music.

"Irish Musicians", a dry-point engraving by Gertrude Degenhardt (1986).

unnerved by the changes of the last twenty years or so, as though they suspect that they may be losing some of the old, relaxed ways and turning into a busy, urgent people much like anyone else. Perhaps they should not worry. Most visitors don't notice. Most continue to remark on the exceptional friendliness and helpfulness of Irish people. And, despite the odd eyesore here and there, the countryside is still very beautiful.

Dublin is a town with two faces: one of them has an aristocratically reserved look, like here in Drury Street, with its brick buildings, influenced by English architecture ...

Dublin

The Irish capital lies on the River Liffey, which flows along under Halfpenny Bridge, divides the city into two and finally turns into Anna Livia Plurabelle: the goddess, beauty and dream figure in James Joyce's *Finnegans Wake*. Dublin may be the capital with the smallest budget for art within the European Community, have the largest number of unemployed, yet it was European City of Culture in 1991, opened a splendid Writers' Museum the same year and in the Temple Bar area, just to the south of the river in the city centre, has one of the most vibrant arts areas in any city in Europe. Not the least of its attractions is something completely unique: the Ark, an arts centre completely devoted to children, with a theatre in which the seats are child-sized and which can stage performances either indoors or outdoors, depending on the season.

The city started as a Viking trading post over a thousand years ago. Lying on the east coast, with a reasonably good navigable port, it was a centre for commerce with Britain from earliest times. Later, once the Normans had established themselves, Dublin quickly

... and the other one full of joie de vivre, as a town of almost Mediterranean energy and love of life, where many activities take place in the open.

became the centre of the royal administration and effectively the capital of the country, a position it has retained to this day.

It is a young city. It contains about a third of the total population of the Republic of Ireland, demographically the most unusual in Europe in that the majority is under thirty. There are young people everywhere. This is reflected in the shops, the clubs and pubs, and the sense of vitality and creativity that are a feature of the city centre.

The main street is O'Connell Street, just north of the river, dominated by the General Post Office, outside which the Irish Republic was first proclaimed during the Rising of 1916. But the fashionable quarter is on the south side of the Liffey, running from Trinity College along Grafton Street to St Stephen's Green and the nearby Georgian squares. This is where you find the most expensive hotels, stores and restaurants, as well as the best-preserved features of the city's architectural heritage.

The oldest part of the city lies slightly to the west of this area, near the castle and the two cathedrals of Christ Church and St Patrick, both of them originally medieval, but heavily restored in the nineteenth century.

One of the most important things about Dublin is its location at the head of the Liffey, where it flows out into the great semi-circle of Dublin Bay. One of the best ways to see the bay is by DART (Dublin Area Rapid Transport) train, which runs right around the curve of the bay from Howth in the north to Bray in the south. There are three city-centre stations, at Connolly, Tara Street and Pearse stations.

Finally, remember that Dublin is a walking city. Most of the sights that visitors want to see are within a short distance of the centre. So take a stroll.

The Church - Religion in the past and today

Almost 80 per cent of all Irish people, and over 90 per cent in the Republic, acknowledge the Catholic faith. That is not just passively so. One need only visit the churches once during Mass to be persuaded how intensely the Irish - men and women alike - live by their faith, which they have defended against all hostile attacks through the centuries. The Church here in Ireland is as powerful as it is in Poland and for the same reason: it is a badge of national identity. Attitudes are changing, however, and people are questioning the authority of the clergy.

The Holy Mountain of the Irish is called Croagh Patrick. On the last Sunday in July many thousands of Irish faithful go on a pilgrimage up to the top of the 2500 feet high rock, on which Ireland's patron saint, St. Patrick, is supposed to have fasted for 40 days, in the year 441. In 1989 it was discovered that the mountain conceals a gold mine. The value of the precious metal is put at around £360 million. Nothing would be simpler than to dig for the gold, giving employment in an underdeveloped area. There were objections, however, most of them based on religious grounds - although it is worth noting that a vociferous environmental lobby also added its voice to the protest, introducing a wholly secular note. Still, the church is influential because of the place it holds in people's hearts. Despite the rash of scandals which have surfaced in the 1990s involving fornicating and drunken clergy, together with some horrifying stories of child sex abuse by priests and other religious leaders, the Church still maintains a formidable influence. Legislation to permit contraception was introduced only with the greatest difficulty. A referendum to remove the constitutional ban on divorce only passed by a whisker. Along with Malta, the Republic of Ireland is the only country in Europe where termination of pregnancy is forbidden by law. Every year up to 4,000 Irish women travel to England for an abortion. There are visible signs of change, though. President Mary Robinson has hinted on more than one occasion her support for more extensive freedoms, including in sexual matters.

The *Irish Times* wrote: "We Irish are an incredible people in applying a double standard. We have a law for everything, yet we all do things which are prohibited." Another paradox is that there is no Catholic cathedral in Dublin. The most beautiful example of church architecture in the capital is St. Patrick's Cathedral - the main church of the Anglicans. In Trinity College too, where today thousands of visitors admire the "Book of Kells" - a high point of Celtic art - only Protestant students were admitted until 1873.

If on the one hand many Irish are rebelling against spiritual authority, there are on the other hand as many who are not to be outdone in their zeal and devotion to their faith. As a young priest in Maynooth said: "The Church is very open at present, because we are confronted by a lot of different views through television, and of course the Church cannot stand aside from this. Morally we are no better than any other people. Fashions in morality affect us too, so we must above all look after young people in the cities, because they can grow up without any feeling for belief. They are faced with free love and want to enjoy it as well. Only marriage can provide that, though. Moral laxity is only a passing phase. Even on the continent, people are coming back to values like love, belief, and faithfulness."

The persistent strength of the Catholic Church in Ireland has its roots in history. As we saw earlier, the Reformation failed in Ireland. The reasons for this are varied and the details are still disputed by scholars. But the fact is that neither the Norman nor Gaelic landowners of the sixteenth century accepted the new religion. The English authorities could not allow a situation in which one of their territories was effectively in the hands of their religious enemy, at a time when England was either at war or threatened by the two major continental Catholic powers, France and Spain. No other country in Europe

Continuation page 75

In the Old Library of Trinity College, Dublin a beautiful winding staircase leads from the ground floor up to the long room ...

... and that is where the 1,200 year old Book of Kells is kept. Of the 340 richly decorated pages, a different one is displayed every day.

FISHING IN IRELAND

On a clear Summer's day we set out to discover the famous Irish fishing grounds for ourselves. In the middle of Ireland there seems to be a lake shining forth behind every hilltop, or a small brook gushing forth, or maybe a quietly flowing river. In this country you don't need a fishing permit to try your luck, and the licences for most types of fish and waters are very cheap, or cost nothing at all.

Today let's try fly-fishing. How stubbornly the small tufts of feathers which are used as bait cling on, and how artistically and inventively they are bound together. They have mysterious names such as Lafontaine's Deep, Borger's Sparkle Pupa, Flashback Midge, Orange Quill, Mayfly or Jellyfry Nymph and are original imitations of insects found in nature. We enviously watch the expert sporting fishermen, casting out their rods time and again far out from a boat, and then slowly hauling them in again. The obligingness of our *ghillie*, Harry, knows no bounds. He tells us in just a few words which fly we can catch salmon with, and with which brightly coloured "attrappe" we can outwit the combative wild Irish river trout, and where there are promising places on the lake. And then yes, we finally chug off to try our luck.

Deep sea, in-shore and fresh-water fish in Ireland are among the best which any European country can offer. This is above all down to the unpolluted waters. Generally the season lasts from March until October, and one can go for about forty different types of fish. Among the favourite angling waters are Lough Derg in the Shannon, the Shannon estuary, and the lakes in County Cavan, north west of Dublin, and generally the whole Lake District, in the centre of Ireland. Distinctions are drawn between salmon and trout from so-called *coarse fishing*, which is the search for pike, perch, eels, bream, and tench. Many local anglers are so spoilt for choice that they concentrate exclusively on the "noble" fish, the salmon, but not the other types.

And with that, we are soon on to the next "angling point", sea fishing. Altogether there are sixty controlled stretches of coastline. Going out from the shore, sea perch, pollock, mackerel, sea salmon, butt and flounder, among others, can be caught. From the deep-water boats, which take all those interested to the best fishing grounds, one can also look for the "really big ones" like shark, skate and halibut. In particular the waters off Youghal, Schull in County Cork, and Blacksod Bay in County Mayo are promising for this.

Finally, there is the king of fish, the salmon. The best chance of catching one is in the river Moy. The season lasts from February to October. Many of the waters are privately owned and a licence is needed, which can, however, be obtained on the spot without any trouble.

Ireland has the richest fishing waters in Europe. Hundreds of rivers and lakes, as well as a long coastline, make it an angler's paradise.

Carrick-on-Shannon lies on the upper reaches of the river Shannon. This small town is not just an excellent starting point for pleasure trips in cabin cruisers, but it also serves rowers and canoeists as a support centre for their daily training sessions.

Double spread overleaf: View over Lough Derg, one of the countless lakes on the course of the river Shannon.

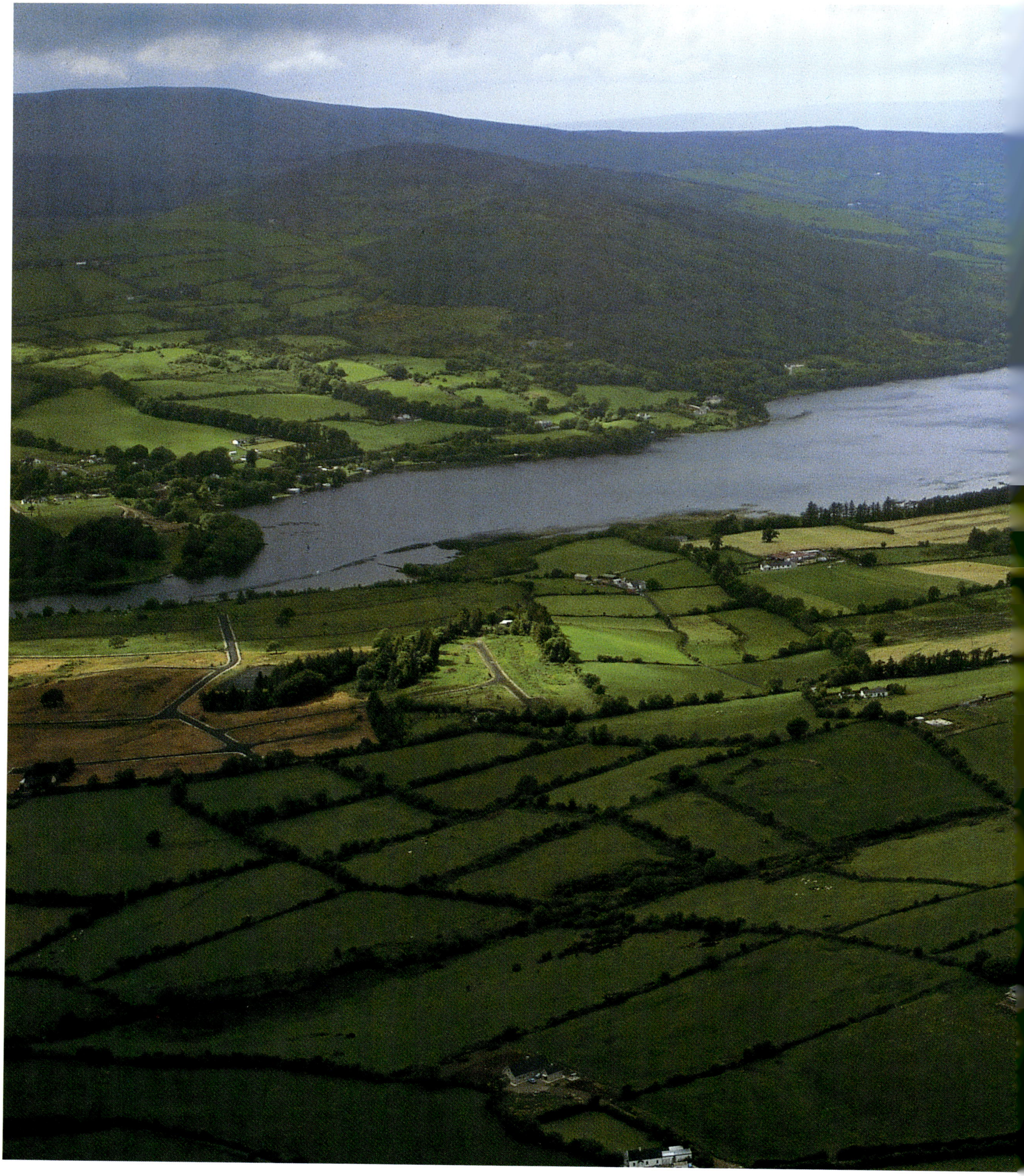

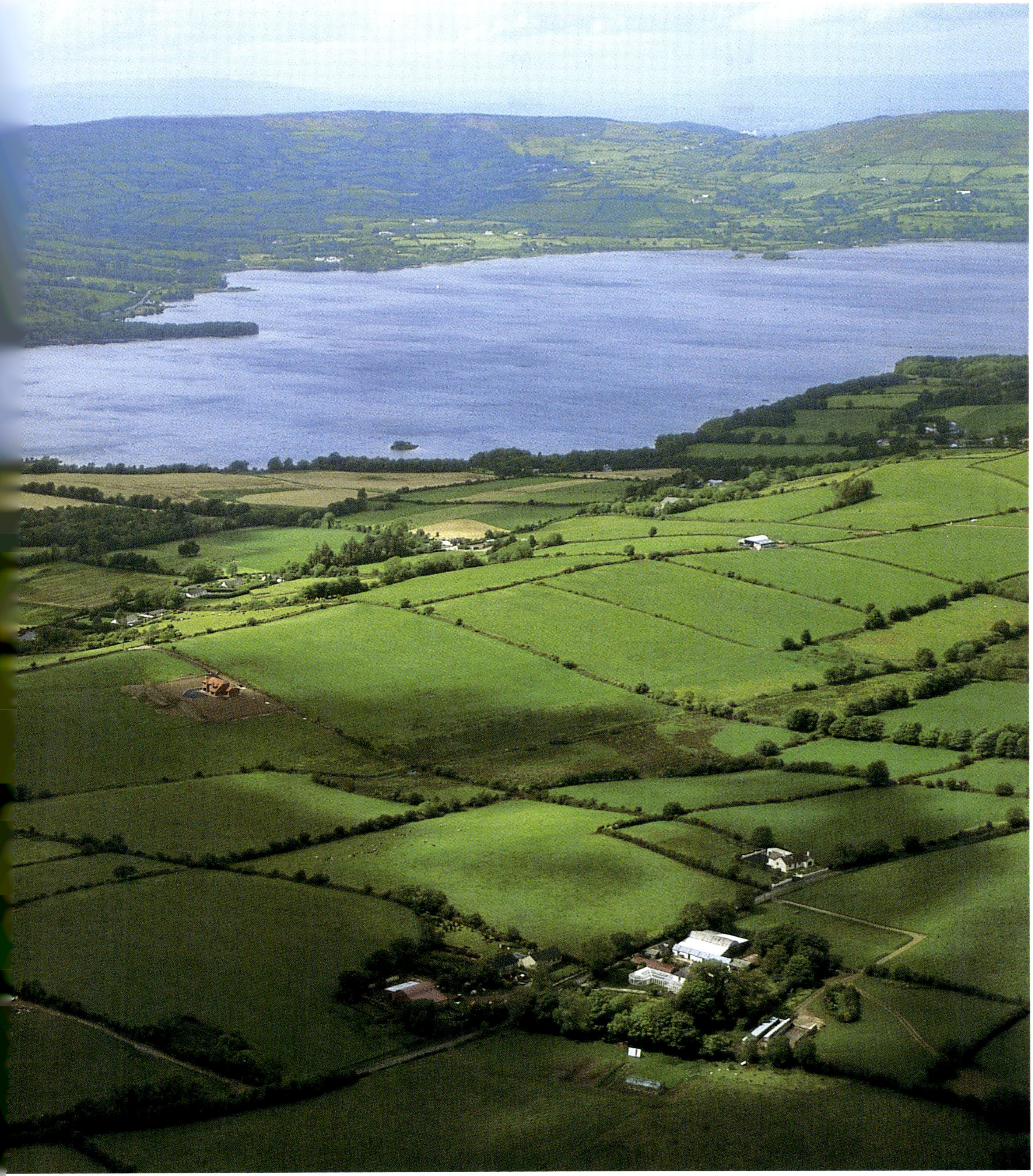

Passing small islands and lonely country houses by, you can reach Carrick-on-Shannon, upstream from the enchantingly situated Lough Key. This reed choked lake is a favourite spot for anglers.

The quieter waters on the upper reaches of the Shannon, such as Lough Key, are in tune with the pace of a tour on a cabin cruiser. Here leisure time skippers can only practise for a little while, before they have to deal with enormous depths and much heavier swell downstream.

Several locks compensate for the differences in height along the course of the Shannon. Anyone exploring the river in a rowing boat or a motor boat must therefore be well practised in the necessary manoeuvres.

In the high season, there may well be traffic jams on some sections of the river and lakes in the Shannon area, as here on Lough Key.

Double spread overleaf: Rain clouds over Main Street in Ballaghaderreen in County Roscommon.

Castlerea
Christy's
RESTAURANT
Mc Governs
INDEPENDENT
SUPERMARKET
Christy's
THE OLD
STAND
AND
Restaurant
OPEN
Breakfast
Served

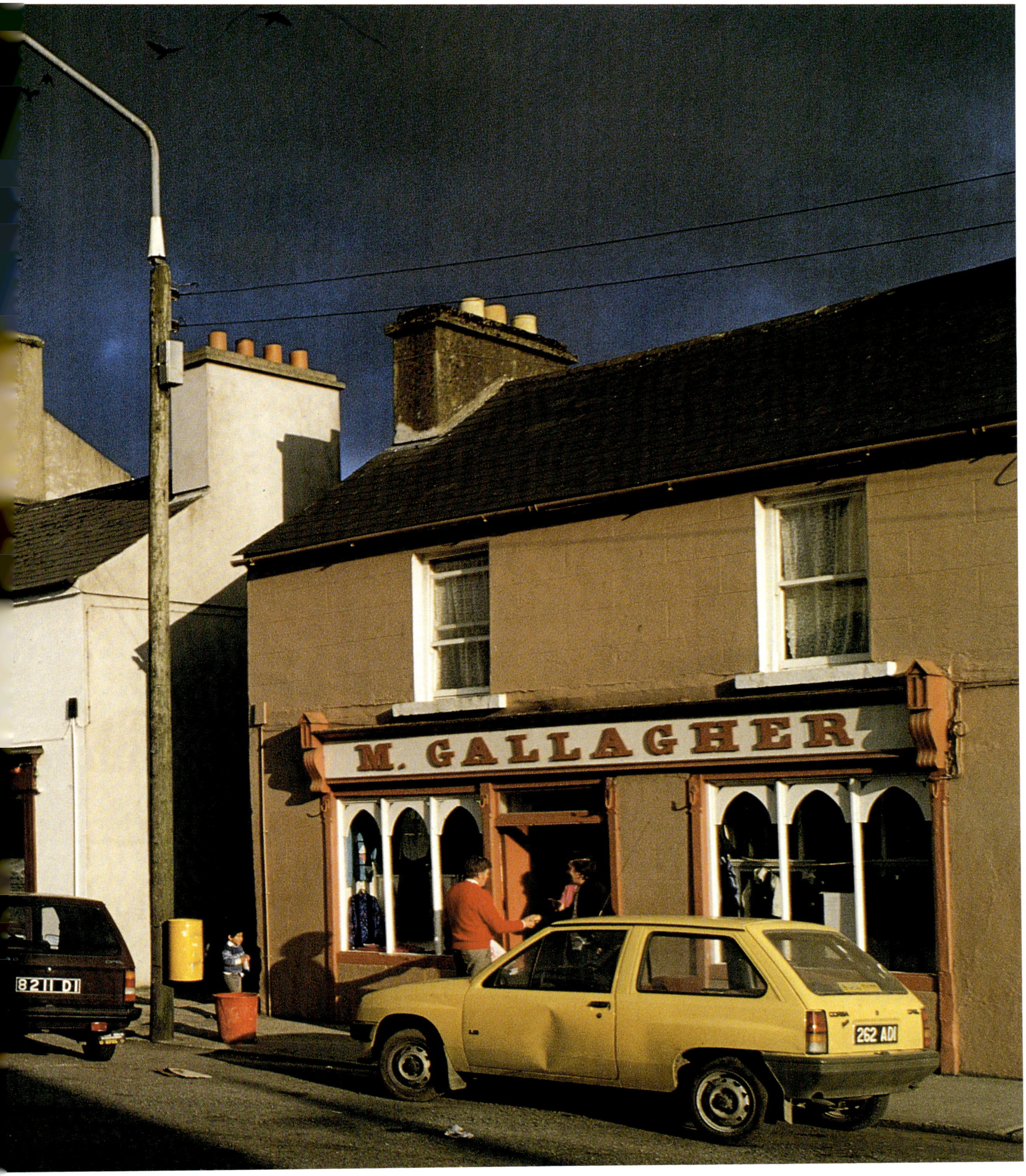
M. GALLAGHER
8211 DI
262 ADI

Lough Derg is not always as peaceful as it appears in this photo. When the wind suddenly increases, high waves can be expected.

permitted this state of affairs. England would either have to fight for full control of Ireland or lose it altogether. The result was a series of English wars of conquest in Ireland, which resulted in the wholesale expropriation of Catholic landowners in the three richest provinces.

By the start of the eighteenth century, all Irish Catholics - whatever their remote origins - now felt the solidarity of the dispossessed. They were still the overwhelming majority of the population, but they were outcasts in their own country. There were legal bars to their advancement and their Church was discriminated against, although not as fiercely as legend later had it. The Church survived. It laid low, bided its time and gradually grew in wealth and confidence. Most of all, it stayed close to the people; it was not an aristocratic Church. So, when Irish nationalism developed in its modern form at the end of the eighteenth century, the Church was one great Catholic institution which was in good order. Its bishops and priests were in position; it had an educational system which produced the new nationalist elite; it had the faith and affection of the common people. It was self-confident, and that self confidence grew through the nineteenth century and into the twentieth. After independence, it became like an established Church - in fact, if not in name - in the Republic. So its recent difficulties, although severe, must be set against that long historical inheritance.

Northern Ireland

Although most Irish landowners from the seventeenth to the early twentieth centuries were Protestants of British stock, they were for the most part surrounded by an overwhelmingly Catholic population. Eventually, in the age of democracy, numbers told. But Ulster was different, at it has always been.

Of all the Irish provinces it was the one with the best natural defences, a series of lakes and low hills called 'drumlins' which kept it safe from invasion from the south for most of its history. Indeed, its relations with Scotland by the seaward route were usually easier than those with the rest of Ireland by the landward route. Thus, by the late sixteenth century, it had most successfully avoided the attentions of the English regime based in Dublin and was the most Gaelic part of the country. Within ten years, with the defeat and flight of the Gaelic chiefs, it became the least so.

The English and Scots planters who were settled in Ulster in the early seventeenth century were not just landowners, but entire communities. From the start Ulster Protestants were numerous. For much of that century they lived in fear of a Catholic backlash. This came in the rebellion of 1641, still remembered as a time of treachery and massacre, and again in the war at the end of the century. The decisive battle of that war, the Battle of the Boyne, saw the Protestant King William III defeat the king whom he ousted, the Catholic James II (the last Catholic to occupy the English throne) on 12 July 1690. It marked the final defeat of Catholicism in the long wars of religion. It is a date still celebrated among Northern Ireland Protestants as their day of deliverance.

Why has little happened to soften the harsh dichotomy of Ulster over three centuries? Basically, because Protestants and Catholics want different and opposite things at any given time. By the middle of the nineteenth century, as Irish Catholics generally were espousing nationalism, Ulster Protestants feared that they would be left as a regional minority at the mercy of the Catholic majority on the island overall. Moreover, as most of nationalist Ireland was suffering the horrors of the Famine, Protestant Ulster was booming, thanks to the industrial revolution, reinforcing an ancient Protestant belief in the poverty and helplessness of the Catholic natives.

All this came to a head as nationalist Ireland moved towards independence in 1922. The country was finally partitioned, but a sizeable Catholic minority was left on the

The picturesque Viking settlement of Strangford lies on the extreme southern end of the Lough of the same name, in the North of Ireland.

Protestant side, in what was now called Northern Ireland. The old Protestant insecurity burst forth in a welter of discrimination against Catholics, in jobs, housing and employment. For almost fifty years Northern Ireland was run by a developed parliament in Belfast as a Protestant fortress.

By 1968 the Catholics had had enough. At first a civil rights movement tried to get normal British standards applied in what was, after all, a part of the United Kingdom. But soon the situation had deteriorated into violence and the Troubles had begun. On the Catholic side, the IRA conducted a terrorist campaign in support of a British withdrawal and Irish reunification. The campaign has achieved little except further to widen the gulf between the two sides in Northern Ireland, if that were possible. Meanwhile, militant Protestants had responded in kind, being responsible for some of the most depraved and mindless killings of the Troubles. By the mid 1990s exhaustion and a growing sense of futility on all sides at the hopelessness of the violence had bought the possibility of lasting peace. But the way ahead is strewn with difficulties, given the malign historical legacy of mutual incomprehension and suspicion.

There is another Northern Ireland though, one which is untouched by the Troubles. Around the wooded island world of Lough Erne, in the sparsely populated County Fermanagh is a paradise for those tired of civilisation, where sailing boats peacefully perform their turning and tacking manoeuvres, anglers watch out for salmon, and hikers visit early Celtic and Christian monuments. Or there is the coast of Co. Antrim facing Scotland, the empty beaches of Ballintoy, the Giant's Causeway, which is a 60 million year old basalt formation, consisting of 40,000 pillars; and there are bathing resorts like Portstewart and Portrush, with fine, safe beaches and the clear, unpolluted surf of the North Atlantic.

This manor house with an almost oriental look is right on the Antrim coast, near Port Ballintrae, in Northern Ireland.

From this land of rugged contrasts, the road goes past the frontier post near Creaghanroe, back into the peaceful Republic. The towers of both the cathedrals in Armagh disappear into the mist. However murderously both faiths have fought on the streets, the churches both have their origins in that county. They have never been a mirror image of Ireland's divisions. It was in Armagh that Ireland's patron saint, Patrick, began his missionary work on the island.

Literature

A respect for writing, learning and poetry goes a long way back in Ireland. In Celtic Ireland poets were an aristocratic caste who passed an oral tradition of literature from one generation to the next. The earliest surviving poems date from the eighth century. But the tradition is much more ancient. The most famous epic of Celtic Ireland is the *Tain Bo Cuailnge (Cattle Raid of Cooley)*, which was itself part of an immemorial oral tradition when it was first written down.

Although Gaelic Ireland was an underdeveloped culture - it had little in the way of painting, sculpture or architecture, perhaps because it was entirely rural and pastoral - its tenacious devotion to poetry and music was among its most distinctive and enduring qualities. This continued through the medieval period. Gaelicised Normans like Gerald FitzGerald, 4th Earl of Desmond, introduced contemporary French conventions of courtly love poetry to the Irish language. But the series of disasters that befell Gaelic Ireland from the sixteenth to the eighteenth century fractured the continuity of the ancient tradition. Although there is to this day a vigorous literature in Irish, it is no longer central to Irish literary culture.

That centrality now belongs to work in English, as it has done for at least 200 years.

Continuation page 84

Belfast 1992: Police and soldiers in front of the headquarters of Sinn Fein, the political party associated with the IRA.

"Orangeman's Day" in Portadown, Northern Ireland. Militant Protestants are still celebrating after 300 years, the victory of the protestant King William III of Orange over the Catholic James II, in 1690.

Belfast in August 1914. Many Irishmen thought their cause would best be served if they fought in the British army as volunteers.

The island of writers: Left: Oscar Wilde (1854 - 1900), and right: George Bernard Shaw (1856 - 1950)

James Joyce (1882 - 1941) on the left, and William Butler Yeats (1865 - 1939)

Samuel Beckett 1906 - 1989) left, Brendan Behan (1923 - 1964) centre, and Sean O'Casey (1880 - 1964) right.

Jonathan Swift (1667 - 1745), the author of Gulliver's Travels.

Double page overleaf: Achill Island. The beautiful countryside has proved an inspiration for many of Ireland's finest writers.

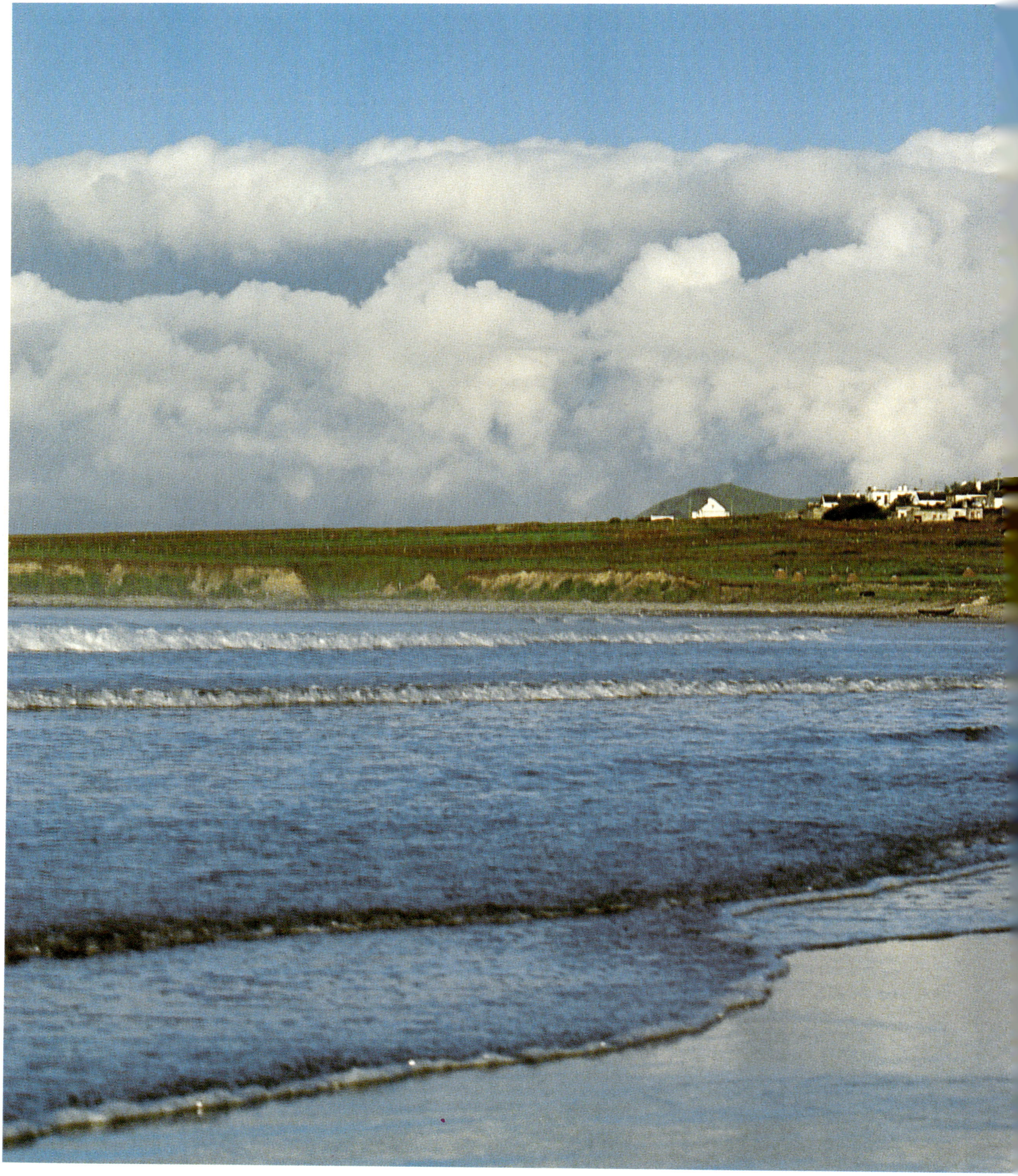

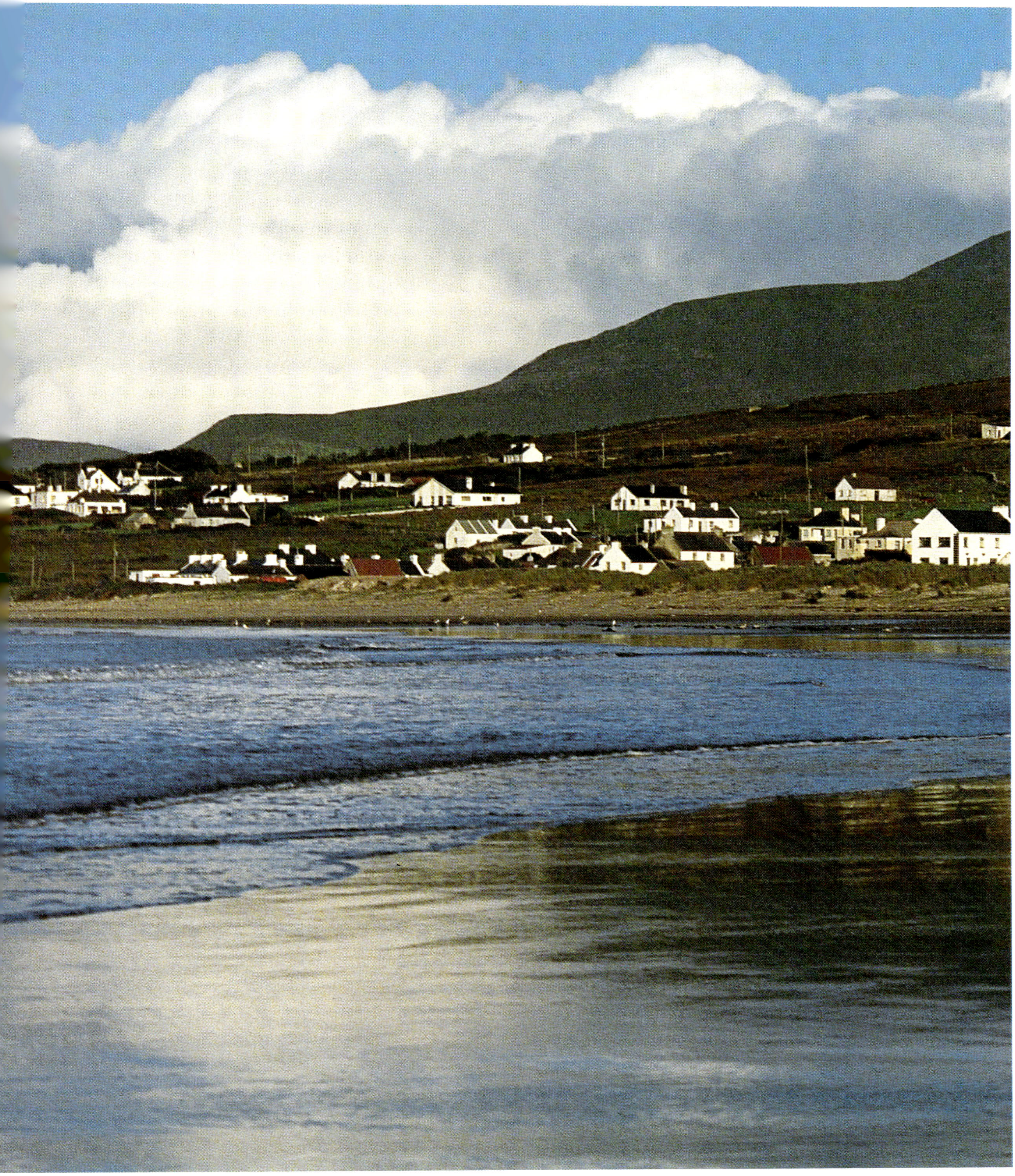

Irish writing in English can be divided into two broad streams. The first is specifically Anglo-Irish, the work of writers from the colonial tradition who, although born in Ireland (and occasionally, as with Swift, living there with the greatest reluctance), had their ambitions focused firmly on London. Dramatists as far apart in time as Farquhar, Congreve, Goldsmith, Sheridan, Shaw and Wilde fall into this category, as does Edmund Burke.

The second stream is that of writers whose direct concern with specifically Irish themes was more pronounced. One first discerns it in the *Irish Melodies* of Thomas Moore, hugely popular in the nineteenth century. There followed a number of minor writers in this tradition, of whom James Clarence Mangan was probably the most accomplished, and then came W.B. Yeats.

Yeats was not only a genius, one of the greatest of all poets, but also the central figure of the Irish Literary Revival. What was being revived was the idea of Irish experience as a proper subject for writers, rather than a cosmopolitan or metropolitan experience. Thus Wilde, for all his brilliance, was never part of the revival in the way that his near contemporary John Millington Synge was. Synge's successor as the leading Irish playwright was Sean O'Casey, a controversial and turbulent man whose fraught relationship with his native country lead to his living the second half of his life in England.

Ireland's most famous literary exile was not impressed by the literary revival, yet no one ever put more of any place into his work than James Joyce did of Dublin. He once boasted that, if the city were destroyed, it could be rebuilt from a close reading of *Ulysses*. This great book - in the opinion of many the greatest novel in any language - is the crowning achievement of Irish literature.

Yeats and Joyce were the twin pillars of Irish writing and after their deaths there was an inevitable hiatus, as other writers felt oppressed by the magnitude of their achievements. Yet poets like Patrick Kavanagh and Austin Clarke, and the novelist Flann O'Brien all produced distinguished work in that time. But the period from the mid 'sixties on has seen a new efflorescence. The outstanding figure is the poet Seamus Heaney, who in 1995 became Ireland's fourth Nobel Prize winner.

I wrote earlier that there are two discernible streams in Irish writing in English. Perhaps that should read "were", because the two have increasingly flowed together as the twentieth century has progressed. The major figure here is Samuel Beckett, an utterly unique voice both as novelist and playwright. No one has written of the emptiness and hopelessness of life with greater power or - by a nice paradox - with greater wit. To miss Beckett's humour is to miss the man. Among contemporary poets, Derek Mahon is reckoned second only to Heaney (many would reverse the order): he, too, is less dependent on specifically Irish locales for his themes, as is also the case with John Banville, the leading contemporary novelist.

Bunratty Castle, between Limerick and Ennis, visible against the night sky. This fifteenth century castle has been lovingly restored and fitted out with contemporary furnishings. Every evening, medieval spreads are laid on in the banqueting hall, for holiday visitors.

Double page overleaf: The small town of Corrofin, surrounded by lakes and the river Fergus is a popular spot for fishing.

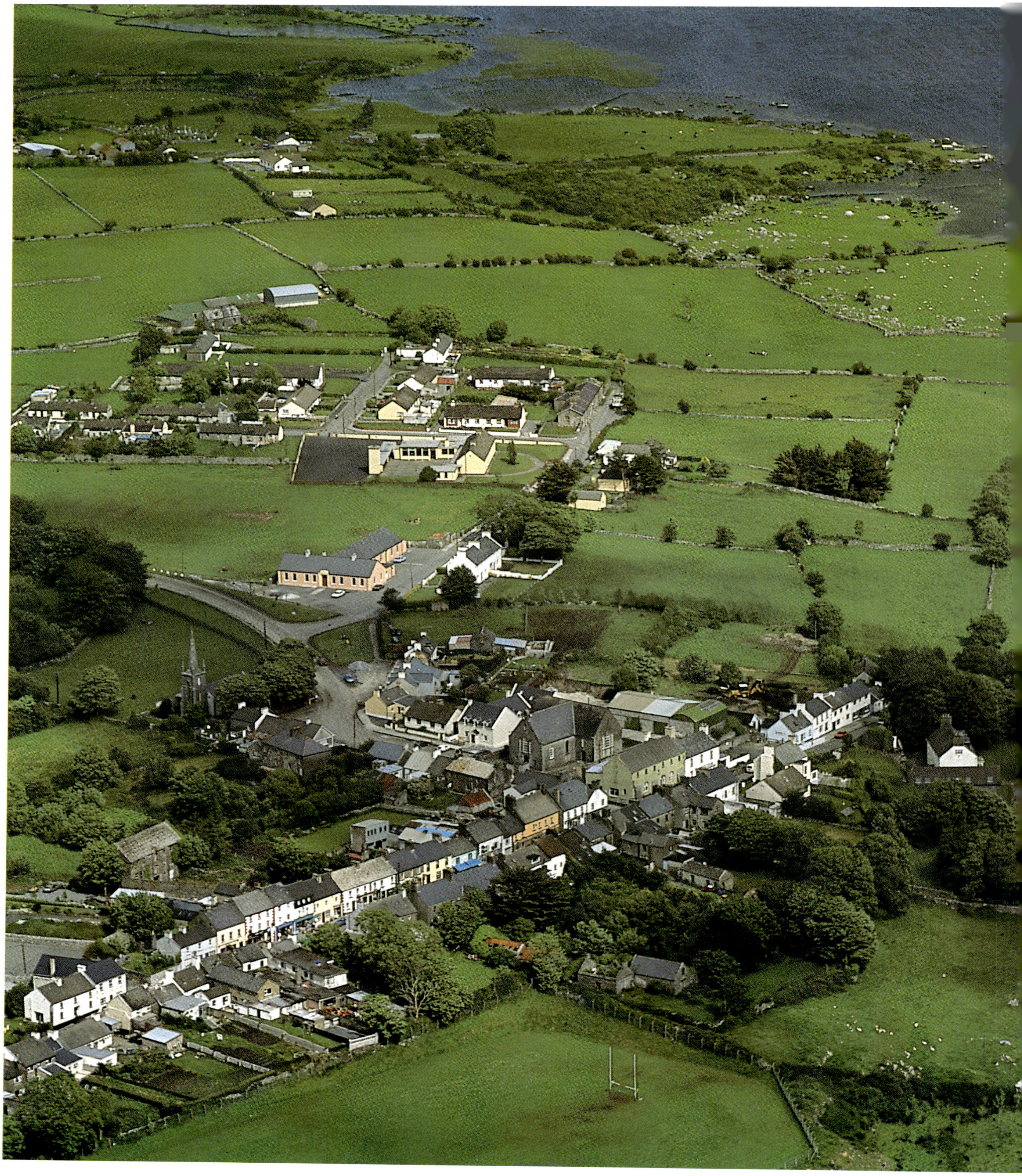

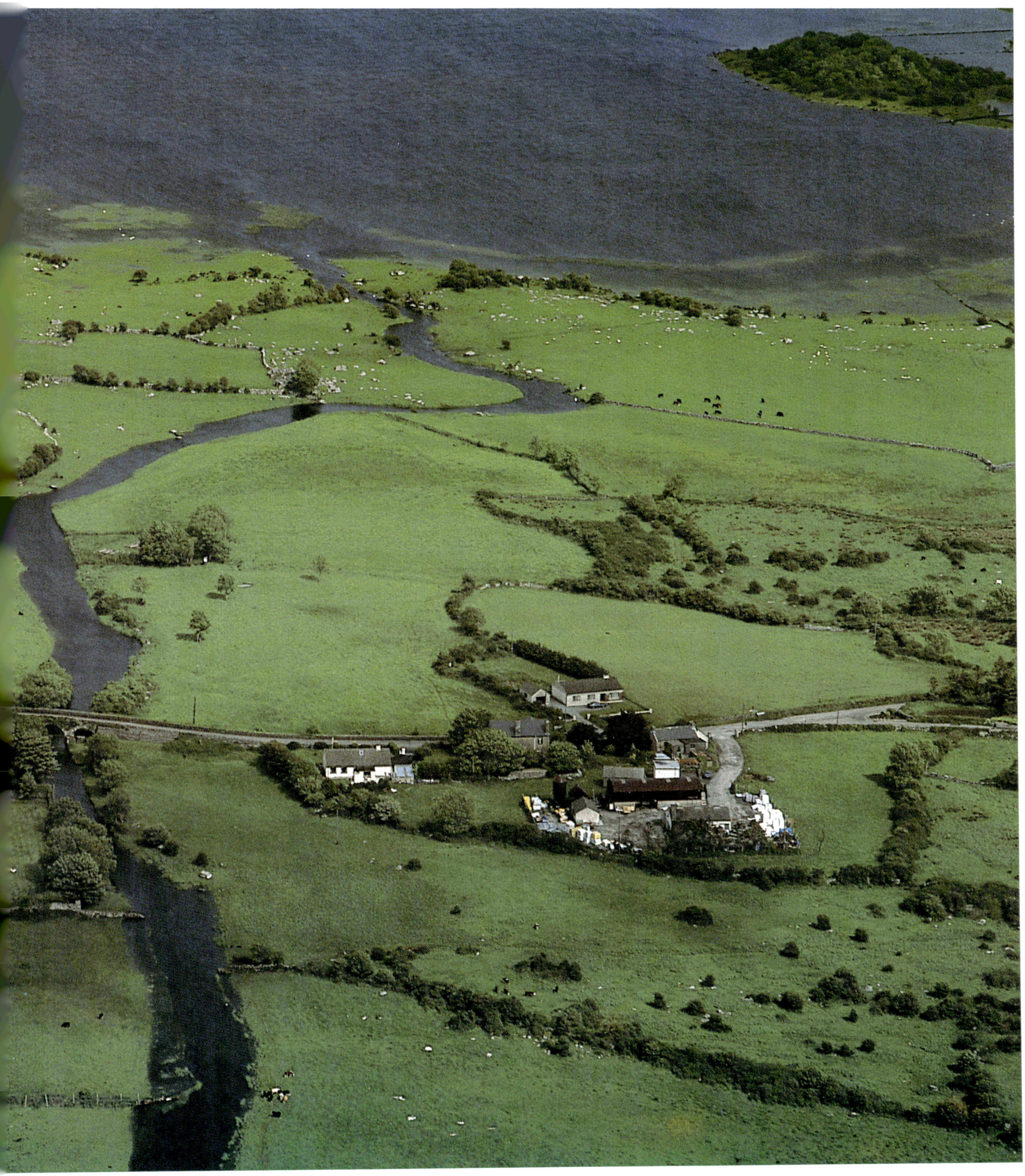

Dún Aenghus lies surrounded by a breathtaking landscape. The magnificent stone fort built in an overpowering semicircle stands at the edge of the sheer Inishmore cliffs, about 300 feet high, above the raging surf.

Dún Eochaill, built with two concentric ring walls, is among the best preserved prehistoric fortress buildings on Inishmore.

The Cliffs of Moher in Co. Clare are the highest and most impressive in Ireland. In clear weather conditions, it is possible to see as far as the Aran Islands from O'Brien's Tower (foreground).

The harbour in the popular resort of Lahinch, on Liscannor Bay.

Double page overleaf: Ballyvaughan churchyard, County Clare.

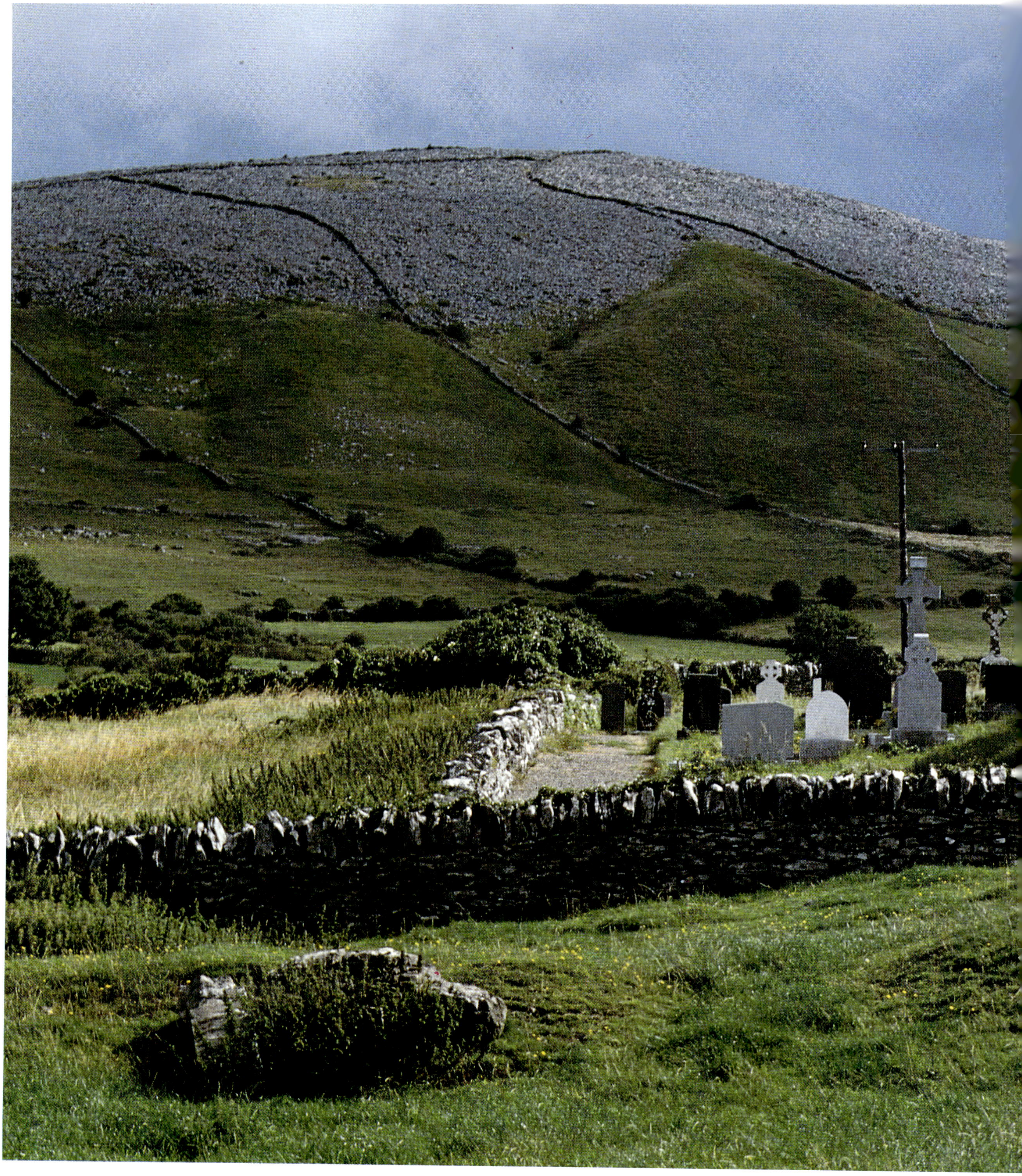

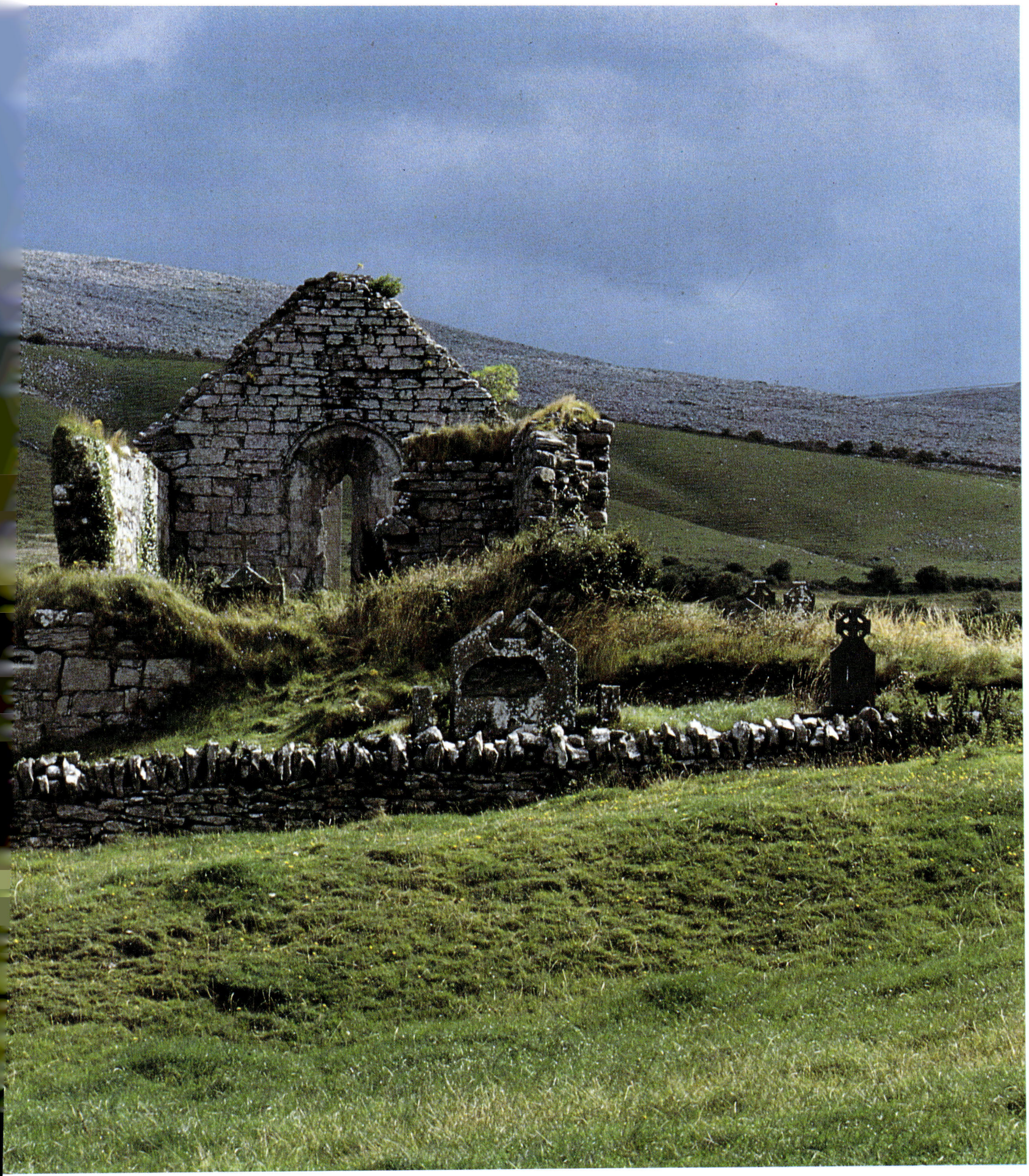

The "Manor House" in Bunratty Folk Park. In this open air museum, several typical Irish buildings have been reconstructed, true to the originals. In them one can watch craftsmen at work, and get a very good impression of Irish rural life in the past.

In the Maam Cross area in Connemara peat is still cut even today, and used as fuel. After cutting, the "bricks" have to be left for a long time to dry in the air.

The landscape around Louisburgh is idyllic. Mountains, rivers teaming with fish, and a coastline with cliffs and sandy beaches all combined in a small area.

Double page overleaf: Typical landscape around Lough Corrib, in County Galway. Stone walls form boundaries on almost treeless and shrubless meadows used as pasture land for sheep.

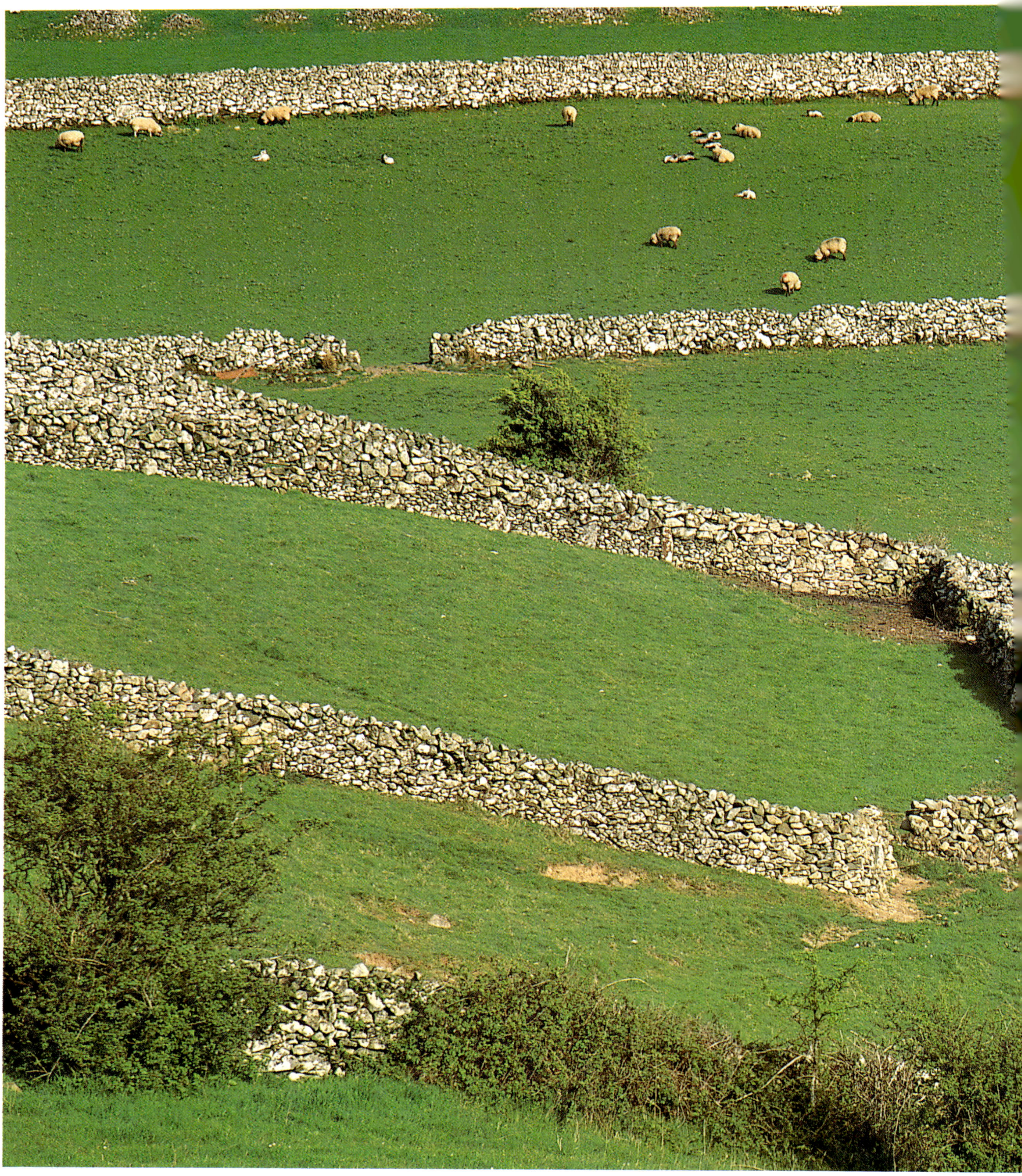

95

On the isthmus between Lough Mask and Lough Corrib, both of them rich fishing grounds, lies the pretty village of Cong. This is where the Gaelic chieftain, Roderick O'Connor, died in 1198.

From the fishing village of Doolin fast boats travel daily to Inisheer, the smallest of the Aran Islands.

Unadulterated Irish provincial life: Near Ballina, in County Mayo isolated whitewashed houses form little coloured specks in the rugged landscape of the north west.

Double page overleaf: Near Letterfrack. The interior of Connemara is sparsely populated and lonely. The "Twelve Bens" can be seen in the background. The highest peak is Benbaun, at about 2500 feet.

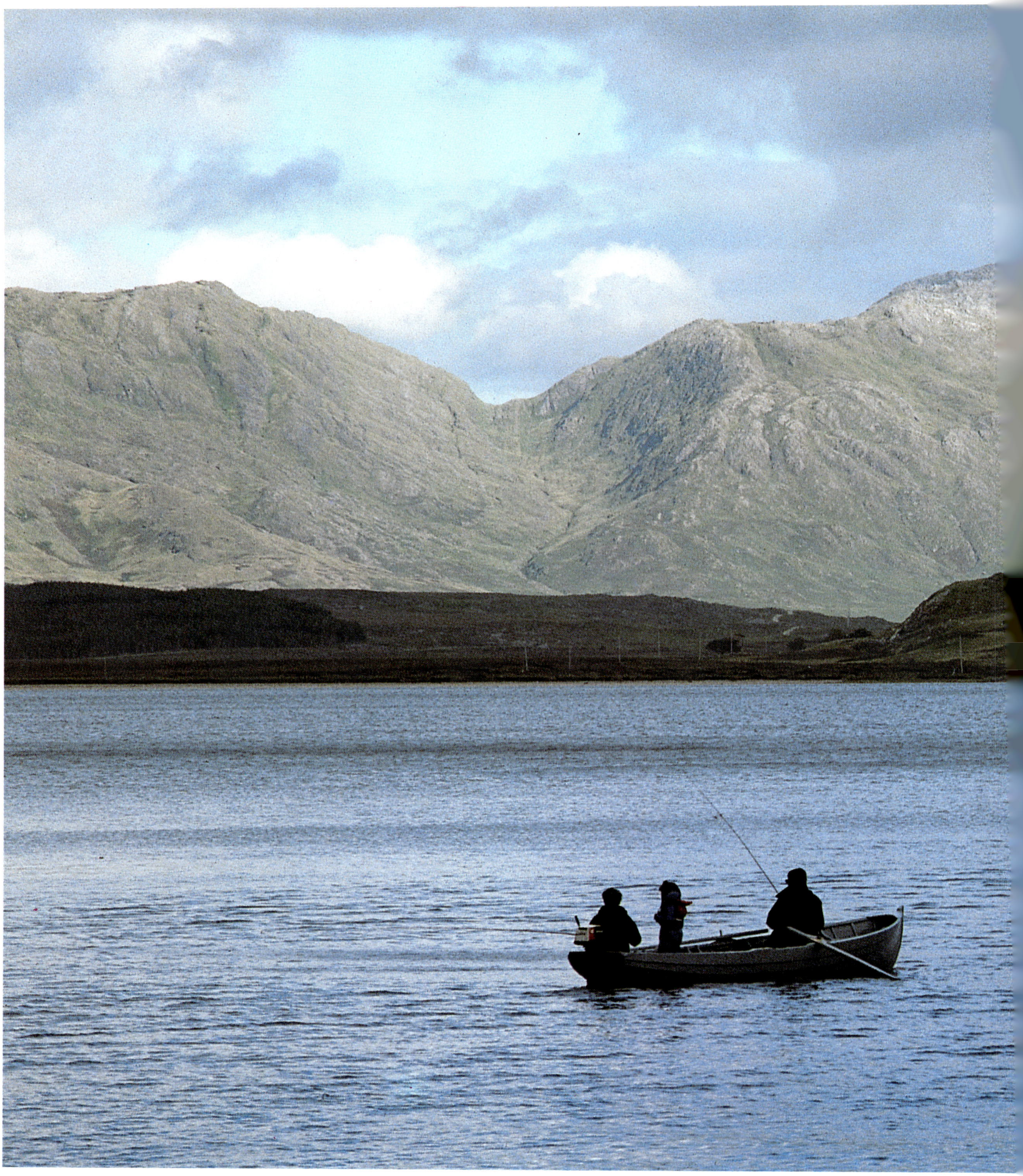

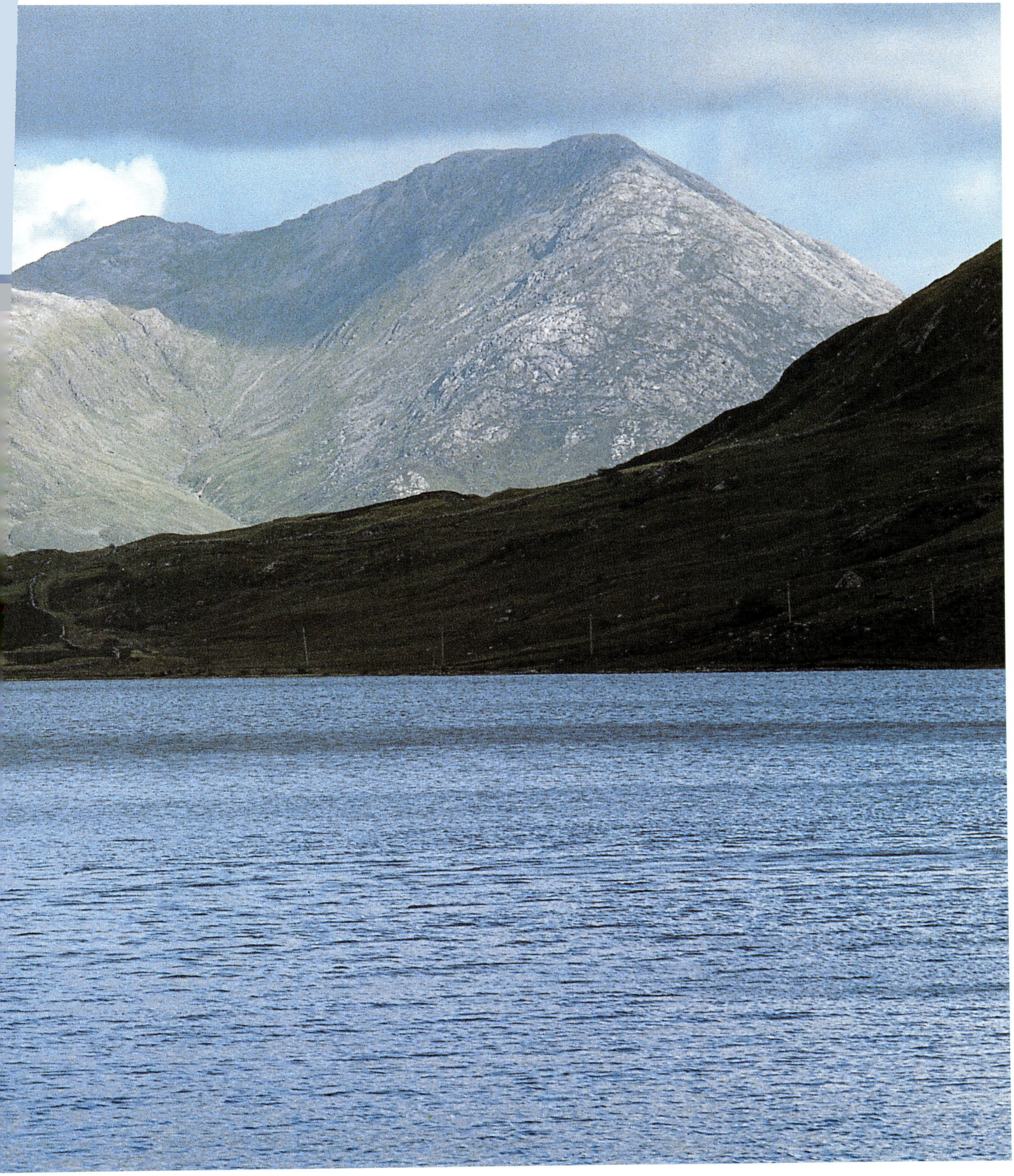

This magnificent sandy beach stretches for 2 miles at Keel, on Achill Island.

Travel Guide through Ireland

Contents

In the land of lakes and green hills 101
The weather: sometimes rain, sometimes sunshine .101
Ireland and its people 102
Political life 102
Two languages - English and Gaelic 104
Irish exports:
Milk, mackerel, and people 104
On the road in Ireland 105
Something for everyone:
"Bed and Breakfast" or Manor House 108
Travel to and around Ireland 108
(Nearly) always with potatoes 108
Things to take home with you 108
Celebrating feast days as they come 108

Routes through Ireland: six suggestions 125
Route map 127
Route 1: From Dublin into the heart of the island ...125
Route 2: Through the wilds of Connemara to the mountains of Mayo 125
Route 3: Ireland in miniature 127
Route 4: On the way to the westernmost point in Europe 128
Route 5: Along the coast of Northern Ireland 128
Route 6: A journey through Donegal, the lonely, wild North West 130
A to Z of tourist attractions and landscapes 131
In the land of racing and betting fanatics 134
Street map of Dublin 148
Map of the river Shannon 152
Being a pleasure boat skipper on the Shannon 153
Map of Ireland 155

In the land of lakes and green hills

Ireland, which lies to the west of Great Britain, currently has a population of about 5 million. The whole west coast is surrounded by the Atlantic Ocean, and in the south - between Wales and the island, there is the strait called St. George's Channel; in the north the North Channel separates Ireland and Scotland; between them is the Irish Sea. The greatest north-south distance is over 300 miles, and the average distance from east to west is less than 200 miles. The total length of the coastline is approximately 1,700 miles. The highest peak is Carrantuohill, at 3,415 feet; at 230 miles long, the Shannon is the longest river, and Lough Neagh the largest lake at 153 square miles.

In Ireland, where the ebb and flow of the tide is very marked, and there is a difference of around 20 feet even on the East coast. The western coastline is strongly indented by bays which reach deep into the land. There are countless sandy beaches and bays in between the cliffs. One of the most fascinating coastal phenomena is the Giant's Causeway, made up of 60-million-year-old basalt pillars. In what is generally a very hilly coastal landscape there are the Wicklow mountains in the East, also known as the "Garden of Ireland" because of the luxuriant vegetation, which stretch from County Dublin, down to County Wexford. But the highest and most dramatic mountains are on the west coast,

in counties Cork, Kerry, Galway and Donegal. Ireland's central lowlands have a large number of lakes and rivers which provide rich fishing grounds. This lakeland area is surrounded by hills and a lot of green pasture land. A mixture of granite, limestone, and volcanic rock formations is characteristic of this very varied landscape. Extensive peat bog areas - one of the last large, still intact eco-systems in Europe - are to be found in the West. That is where the pattern of meadows enclosed by stone walls came from too. Among the most impressive areas is the karst landscape of The Burren, where rare plants and flowers, otherwise only found in the Alps or Pyrennees, flourish in the grey limestone. Until well into the eighteenth century the island's woodland was densely covered in oak trees, which were cut down by the English, to build boats for their fleet. This forest clearance occurred on such a large scale that of all European countries, Ireland is now the poorest in woodland. In 1993 the government undertook a reafforestation programme. 30,000 hectares of woodland are to be replanted every year.

The weather: sometimes rain, sometimes sunshine

Compared with America, Ireland's temperature range does not fluctuate widely. The climate, strongly influenced by the warm Gulf Stream, is damp and mild, there are no harsh winters, nor tropical summers. As there is nowhere which is more than 60 miles away from the sea, the inland climate is moderate as well. Daily and annual temperature variations are small due to the moderating influence of the Atlantic, with rainfall all the year round. Snow is rare in the southern half of the island, but night frosts are common in the winter months. In the west average annual rainfall is between 60 and 80 inches, and in the east only 32 inches. When it rains, it usually does so in short, sharp showers, as the wind makes for rapid clearance, and the sun soon reappears. Rainbows in the sky therefore occur frequently. May and June are the sunniest months, with about 200 hours sunshine on average. May, June and September are the months with the lowest rainfall. Spring and Autumn are pleasantly mild. In Summer it is rarely any warmer than 75°F, and because of the particularly favourable location in North West Europe, daylight lasts at least an hour longer than on the European mainland.

Ireland and its people

About half of the 3½ million people who live in the Republic of Ireland are under 25. There are about 1½ million people living in Northern Ireland. The greatest concentration of population is in the greater Dublin area, where almost one in three of the Republic's population live. The rest of the country is sparsely populated. The second largest city is Cork, with about 150,000 inhabitants. With only 50 inhabitants per square kilometre, the Republic is one of the most sparsely populated countries within the European Union.

In ethnic, religious, cultural and linguistic terms the Republic of Ireland is largely homogeneous. Over 90 per cent of the population is Catholic, although actual rates of religious practice have declined in recent years. Northern Ireland, on the other hand, is divided between a Protestant population of about a million which favours the continuation of the union with Britain and a Catholic population of about a half a million which is nationalist and wishes for the reunification of the island as an independent republic. The population numbers have been subject to severe fluctuations in the course of Ireland's tragic and chequered history. In 1841, the population was over 8 million. As a consequence of the severe famine from 1845 to 1849, during which about a million people died, and the mass emigration which it gave rise to, mainly to the USA and Australia, towards the end of the nineteenth century, the population had fallen to half that figure. Between the wars huge numbers of Irish emigrated again to start up a new life elsewhere. By 1961 the population of the island had fallen to 4.25 million. Thanks to the economic upturn of more recent years and the high birth rate, the population is steadily increasing, however, even though about 30,000 young people still emigrate every year, because they see no prospect of finding work.

One group in the population are the *tinkers*, officially called *travelling people*. These Irish nomads are supposedly descendants of the famine poor. The number of *tinkers* is estimated at about three thousand, and they are often seen camping near roadsides. Only rarely do they still travel through the land in their traditional covered waggons, nowadays they own dormobiles and cars.

Anyone who dares look down from the Slieve League cliffs by the sea into the yawning abyss, ought not to suffer from vertigo.

Political Life

Constitutionally speaking, the island consists of two independent parts: the Republic of Ireland (Eire) and Northern Ireland, which belongs to the United Kingdom of Great Britain and Northern Ireland. Dublin is the capital of the Republic, and Belfast the capital of Northern Ireland. Ireland is divided into four provinces: Ulster with nine counties, Leinster with twelve, Connaught with five, and Munster with six counties.

Centuries of occupation by the British have left their mark on the Irish political scene. When the South finally won independence in 1922, six northern counties, with their Protestant majority, remained a part of the UK after threatening a military uprising.

The 'Troubles' of Northern Ireland are dealt with

The Aasleagh Waterfall, not far from Leenane, runs down between broom bushes, pines and rhododendrons in the Killary Gorge.

Wild rhododendrons in flower near Ballina.

briefly elsewhere in this book but as of this writing there is peace at last and hope for a settled future.

After a plebiscite in 1937 Ireland declared itself a Republic based on parliamentary democracy. The Head of State is the President, elected for seven years, with a maximum of two terms of office. In 1973 Ireland became a member of the European Community. In 1990, Mary Robinson became the first woman President. Legislative power rests with the two houses of Parliament, which consists of the lower house with its 166 members, and the upper house with its 60 members. Leinster House in Dublin, built in 1746, is the Parliament building. Members of the lower house are in session four times a year, and the deputies are drawn from 41 constituencies. The highest judicial authority is the Supreme Court in Dublin. There is no compulsory military service in Ireland; the country's defence forces are volunteers.

The Irish flag is a green, white and orange tricolour. Green stands for the Republic, orange for Northern Ireland, and the white is supposed to symbolise peace between them. There are also two other proudly displayed national emblems: the golden harp with silver strings, and the green shamrock.

There is a wide and colourful choice in the Cork market of oysters, crayfish, plaice, hake, ocean perch, salmon, mackerel and herring. Sea fishing, and more recently fish farming, are an important sector of the Irish economy, particularly so in the case of salmon.

Two languages - English and Gaelic

There are two official languages, Irish and English. Gaelic is an old Celtic language, taught in schools though with limited success. An estimated 55,000 Irish people speak Gaelic. English is the majority vernacular, and is spoken everywhere.

Nurturing of the old language is very important to the young republic, as it gives the Irish a feeling of national identity. During the great period of the Celtic and Christian cultures in Ireland, until about the thirteenth century, Gaelic was the national language and the Irish were well-known throughout Europe for their knowledge and learning. To be an Irishman was a mark of distinction, as the Irish brought their culture to the barbarous continent and confirmed them in their faith.

Irish exports - Milk, mackerel, and people

Ireland is an aspiring industrial country. Significant industries are export-orientated: office and computer goods, glass manufacture, machine construction and the chemical industry. Thanks to conditions which are favourable to entrepreneurs (environmental protection measures are less stringent), multi-national pharmaceutical companies have settled here. The foodstuffs and luxury foods industries also have a high turnover. The sharp rise in property prices is a visible sign of prosperity. Yet there are a lot of people unemployed. At present the figure in the Republic is around 20 per cent. There are still large numbers of young Irish people emigrating in the search for work elsewhere. Among them are many graduates, but less educated workers as well, who go mainly to England as seasonal workers earning the lowest wages of about £3.50 an hour.

There are moderate quantities of mineral products in the forms of zinc, copper, lead and silver. The country derives two-thirds of its energy from crude oil, which has to be imported. Strongly export-orientated agriculture also fills an important role in this country, which is short of raw materials. About 85 per cent of the area used for agriculture is devoted to a cattle breeding economy. Predominant are dairy produce such as cheese and butter, and cattle rearing. More than two-thirds of the farms are family businesses with holdings of less than 50 acres. The larger farms are in the eastern half of the country. Sheep farming is pursued mainly in the uplands. Because of intensive use of the ground environmental problems are starting to occur. The soils are nitrate-laden, drainage water runs into the seas and rivers, where fish stocks are threatened.

Among the most important trading partners are Great Britain, the United States and Germany. Fisheries in particular have gained in importance in recent years. Sea fish such as mackerel, herring, cod, plaice and shellfish – among them oysters and mussels – have been successfully marketed. Salmon farming and the sale of wild salmon are particularly lucrative.

On the road in Ireland

Tourism is the most successful growth industry and is a significant source of hard currency. For this the country has to thank not just the friendliness of its inhabitants or the variety of its charming landscape, but also an extremely successful advertising campaign. The annual 3.1 million holidaymakers spend more than 920 million punts on the island. Investment has been just as strong in the infrastructure – building of hotels and holiday homes – as it has been in training employees within the industry. At 1.7 million guests, the largest share comes from Britain. Then come the Americans, the French, the Dutch, and German-speaking visitors.

In recent times more Spaniards and Italians have discovered Ireland as well. Anglers and water sport enthusiasts also travel in large numbers to the land of the rainbow. The build up of holiday homes belonging to many Germans, French and Dutch on the favoured west coast will certainly slow down somewhat in the coming years, as this region has found itself at the threshold of its ecological tolerance level, and one has to say that the environment is threatened by growing population density.

The most popular destinations are the South Coast,

The sheep-shearing season has arrived here, in Louisburgh. Here in the North West, hardly any agricultural use of the land is possible other than sheep rearing, because of the poor soil.

Left, top and bottom: Muckross House, built in 1843, surrounded by particularly beautiful rhododendron gardens, in Killarney National Park. Today it houses a local history, geography and biology museum, but you can also be driven by pony and trap from here to Muckross Lough, with its strange limestone cliffs.

Right: Relaxing in a well-stocked library under a chandelier, and received with a hearty welcome, or having an exquisitely prepared meal in a superb dining room. Former manor houses and homes of the gentry, which have been converted into luxurious hotels, make this possible for the holidaymaker for short periods; this is the case in Adare Manor Hotel, for example (left, top to bottom, and top right), or in Rosleague Manor (bottom right), near Letterfrack.

107

County Wexford in the South East, the Wicklow mountains, Kerry with its three peninsulas, County Donegal and Connemara. The great prehistoric site at Newgrange should on no account be missed. Old monastic sites like Cashel and Glendalough are very popular, as are the River Shannon - you can cruise for 185 km of its length - and the island off the west coast. In Northern Ireland, the Antrim coast near the Giant's Causeway is exceptionally beautiful.

Something for everyone: "Bed and Breakfast" or Manor House. Whatever you are looking for, there is something to suit your taste: from a comfortable suite in a castle to a cosy room in a private house. The available offers are encouraging, sometimes bewilderingly so. The *Accommodation Guide*, a hotel guide with about 250 pages, shows clearly all the available overnight accommodation, including farm houses, youth hostels and camp sites. In addition over 230 houses, each with its unique character, have joined their particular associations, such as the Friendly Homes, Irish Country Homes, Manor House Hotels, Private Irish Country Houses, or Traditional Irish Hotels.

In the case of the *Friendly Homes of Ireland*, these are a selection of small family-run hotels. They range from small cottages to luxury hotels, but the charm and atmosphere is something common to all. *Private Country Houses* target country life enthusiasts. The houses differ from others in that they have no guests' lounge, and the owners live there also. The *Manor Houses* are luxurious establishments, mostly castles, palaces or old manor houses, in which the cuisine is usually magnificent. In the most beautiful of villages are the *Village Inn Hotels*, in which you can not only enjoy the atmosphere of the house, but take part in village life as well. *Coast and Country Houses* are impressive for the range of leisure activities they offer. In Northern Ireland there are camp sites as well, and here too the hotels and guest houses have organised themselves into *Farm and Country Holidays*, among other organisations.

Travel to and around Ireland: As an alternative to travelling in your own car, you can fly to Dublin, Cork, Belfast or Shannon and hire a car there. Motor cycles and mopeds are not available for hire. There are frequent ferries between Great Britain and Ireland. Traffic drives on the left in Ireland. The permitted blood-alcohol level is up to 0.8 pro mille; maximum speeds are 30 m.p.h. in built-up areas, and 55 m.p.h. on country roads (1 mile = 1.6 km). Nearly all petrol stations sell unleaded petrol. Smaller places are connected by frequent bus services (Bus Eireann), while the larger towns are connected by a good railway network (Iarnrod Eireann). There are weekly discount rates such as the Rambler Ticket, which is sold from the National Transport Company, C.I.E.

(Nearly) always with potatoes: Bread, butter, and potatoes are never absent from the Irish diet. On the coasts, a lot of sea food is eaten as well. The lakes, rivers, and the ocean have fish in abundance: oysters, salmon and lobsters are commonly on the menu. Throughout the country, free range meat – beef, pork, lamb – is always on offer. Of course, there is *Irish stew* as well, a mutton stew with carrots and onions. Light snacks are available in pubs. There are three meal times: first the traditional copious Irish breakfast, lunch and the multi-course dinner. The older tradition of a large lunch - the main meal - followed later by tea, a light meal taken at about 6 p.m., still persists in places. All hotels and restaurants offer good value tourist menus, and show the appropriate symbol - a small green shield. People drink a lot of tea and milk, and of course stout. Coffee should perhaps be avoided, though.

Things to take home with you: Smoked salmon is a particularly popular thing to take home. Waterford cut glass is known worldwide. Pipes and silver decoration with traditional "Celtic" shapes and motifs are bought by some, as well. Also much prized are hand-woven tweed from Donegal, traditional knitwear from Aran, uncoloured beige wool, and linen cloth or tablecloths. Tourism has in many ways led to a revival of handicrafts: pottery, basket-making, glasses and lovingly painted pictures, sometimes with subjects from past centuries – they are all there waiting for a buyer. Then there is weatherproof clothing, cassettes with traditional Irish music, musical instruments, antiques and sportsgear. Anglers and golfers can completely re-equip themselves in Cork and Dublin. The *shillelagh* is also a typical item; it is a stick made of blackthorn wood, which the Irish formerly used as a walking stick and as a weapon. When you visit Dublin, the brochure "Essential Guide to Shopping, Dining and Pubs" is recommended.

Celebrating feast days as they come: Every county and every town has its own festival. In Summer many places hold a regular *seisiun*; these are folklore evenings with Irish dancing and music. The local information bureau of the Irish Tourist Board will provide information on these. Among the major events is the National Day, St. Patrick's Day, on 17 March. *Bloomsday* on 16 June attracts all James Joyce enthusiasts and is celebrated in Dublin with a festival of literature. The *All Ireland Fleadh* takes place at the end of August, with traditional music and Irish dancing. Tralee goes through the selection of the *Rose of Tralee* in August, and in Killorglin on the second weekend of the month there is *Puck Fair*, where a wild goat is crowned king. Ballycastle in the North draws the crowds with its *Old Lammas Fair*, as does Galway in late September when the oyster season starts, with its *Oyster Festival*. The most famous horse and pony market on the island is held in the first week in October, with abundant festivities, in Ballinasloe.

Whitewashed houses, surrounded by luxuriantly blooming hedges, are to be found almost everywhere on Achill Island, Ireland's largest offshore island.

Achill Island, with its extensive beaches, sheltered bays and lonely heathland landscapes.

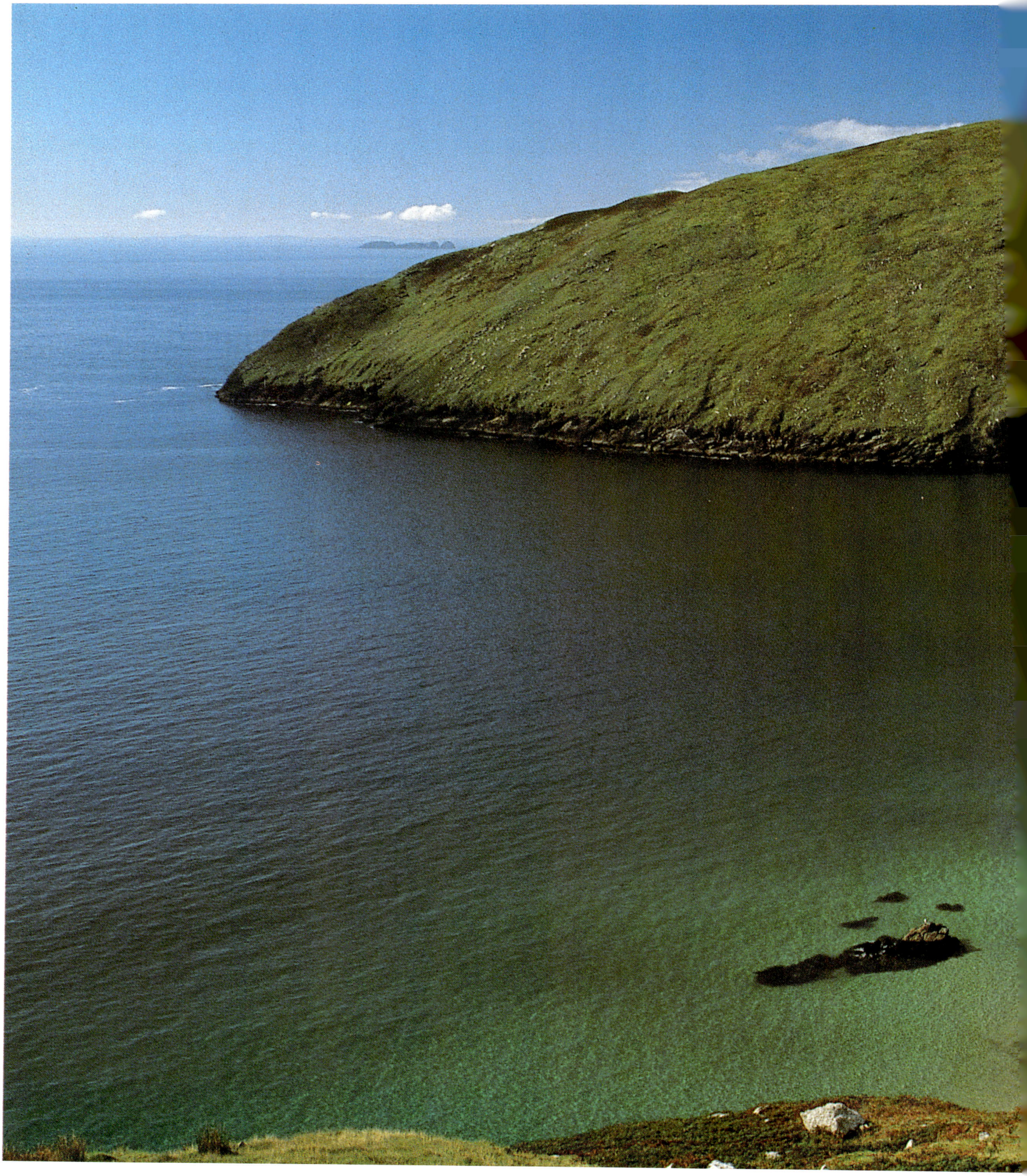

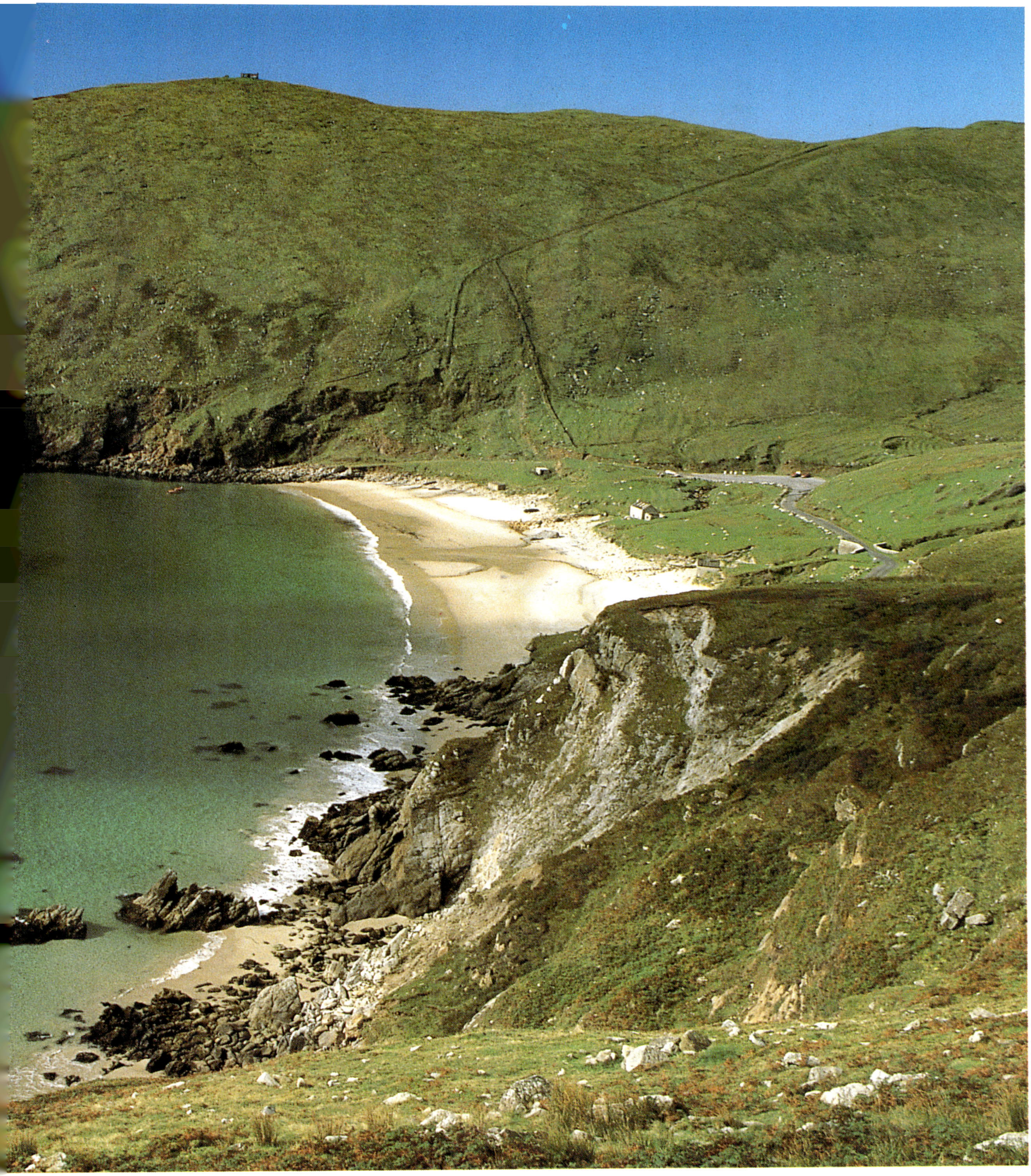

Milford, at the southern end of the fjord-like Mulroy Bay, is a fishing centre. At night the often brightly coloured fishing boats chug out to the fishing grounds and back in the early morning with their nets full.

The mild climate on Achill Island allows abundant growth of vegetation. Fuchsias, rhododendrons, and heathland make this young shepherd's work more pleasant, as he drives his herd out to pasture.

Near Belmullet, County Mayo. The rain here has either just stopped or is about to start.

This pub in Teelin manages perfectly well without a sign. Its arresting colour guarantees it cannot be passed over. Refreshment is available here after an excursion to Slieve League, which is the highest seaside cliff in Europe.

On the Atlantic Circuit, a road running around the Rosguill peninsula in the extreme north of Ireland, is the small town of Downings, a holiday resort with magnificent sandy beaches. The fishermen leave from here for deep sea fishing.

While the signs point the way to other parts some might prefer to bide a while at Biddy's in Cashel.

Boats in the dry dock at Moville on the Inishowen peninsula.

The atmosphere at a traditional cattle auction in Manorhamilton is loud and heated. Whether it is cattle ...

... or sheep, the pride of both the old and the new owner is written all over these men's faces.

Cattle auction in Manorhamilton: While some are still looking with a critical eye at the animals on offer, before making their bid ...

... others talk shop about the breed, milk yield, meat quality and genetic traits.

Double page overleaf: Rathmelton on a creek of Lough Swilly. The fantastic splashes of colour of the blood-red window shutters and doors in these grey surroundings produce an eerily beautiful atmosphere.

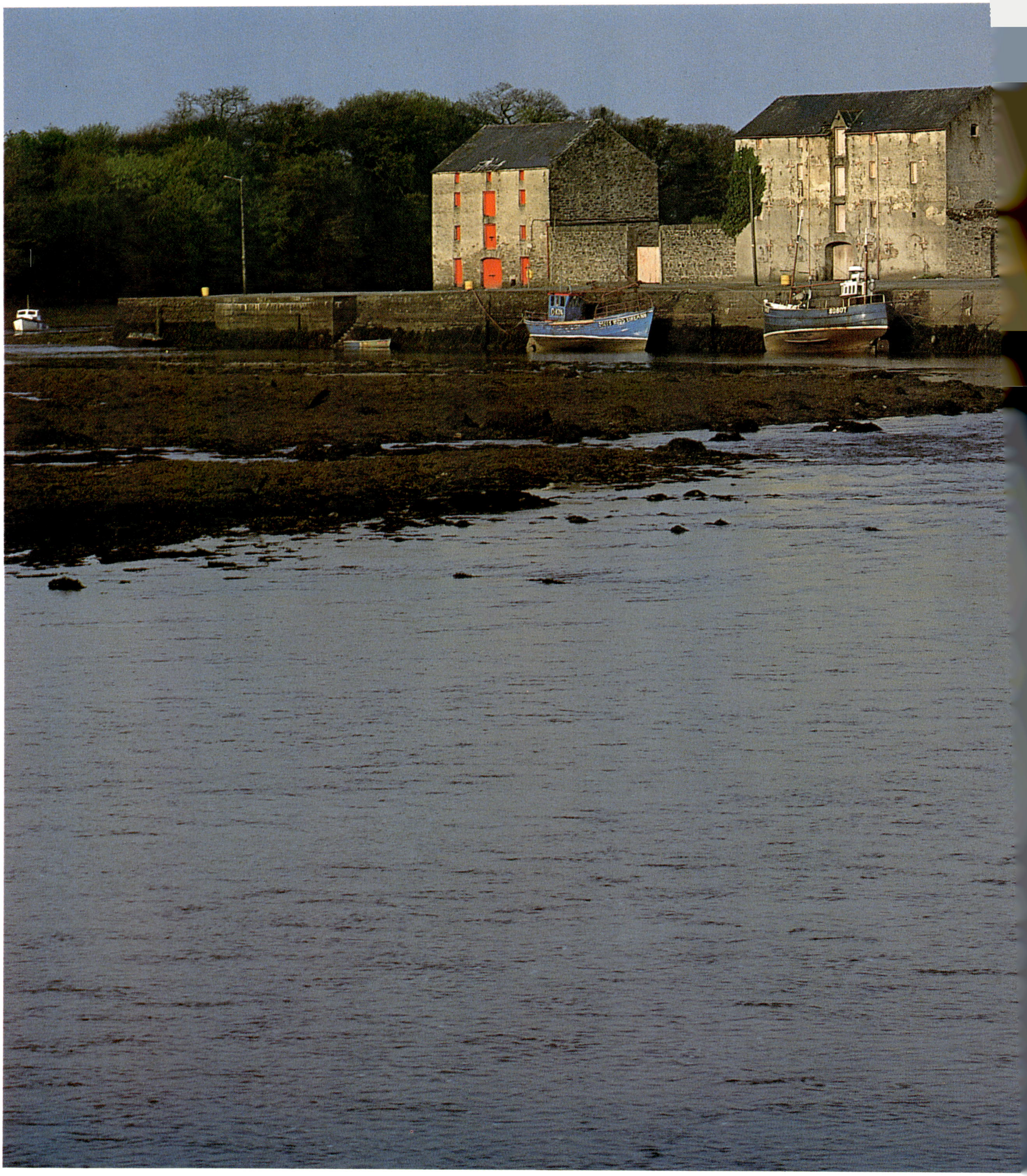

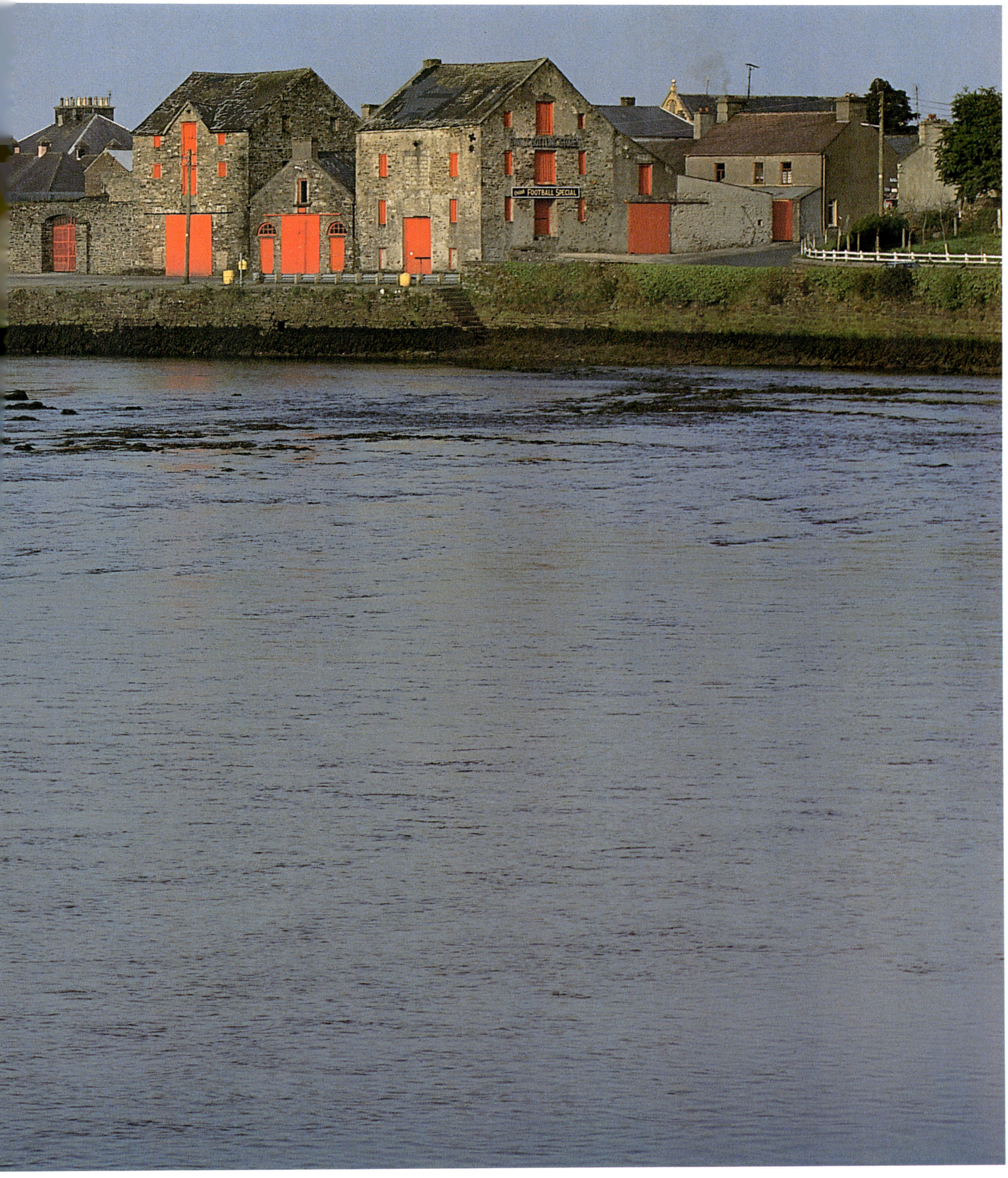
FOOTBALL SPECIAL

The narrow Achill Sound, separates the island from the mainland. It is almost entirely covered by heath and moorland, and the agriculturally viable land is to be found only in the valleys and near the coast. Dreamlike bays ...

... and beaches, such as this one at Keem, attract swimmers and ramblers.

These thatched cottages in Donegal are certainly not the last word in amenities, but they make up for it in inimitable Irish flair.

Double page overleaf: While the west coast of the Mullet peninsula is almost bare, on the east side green meadows surround Blacksod Bay.

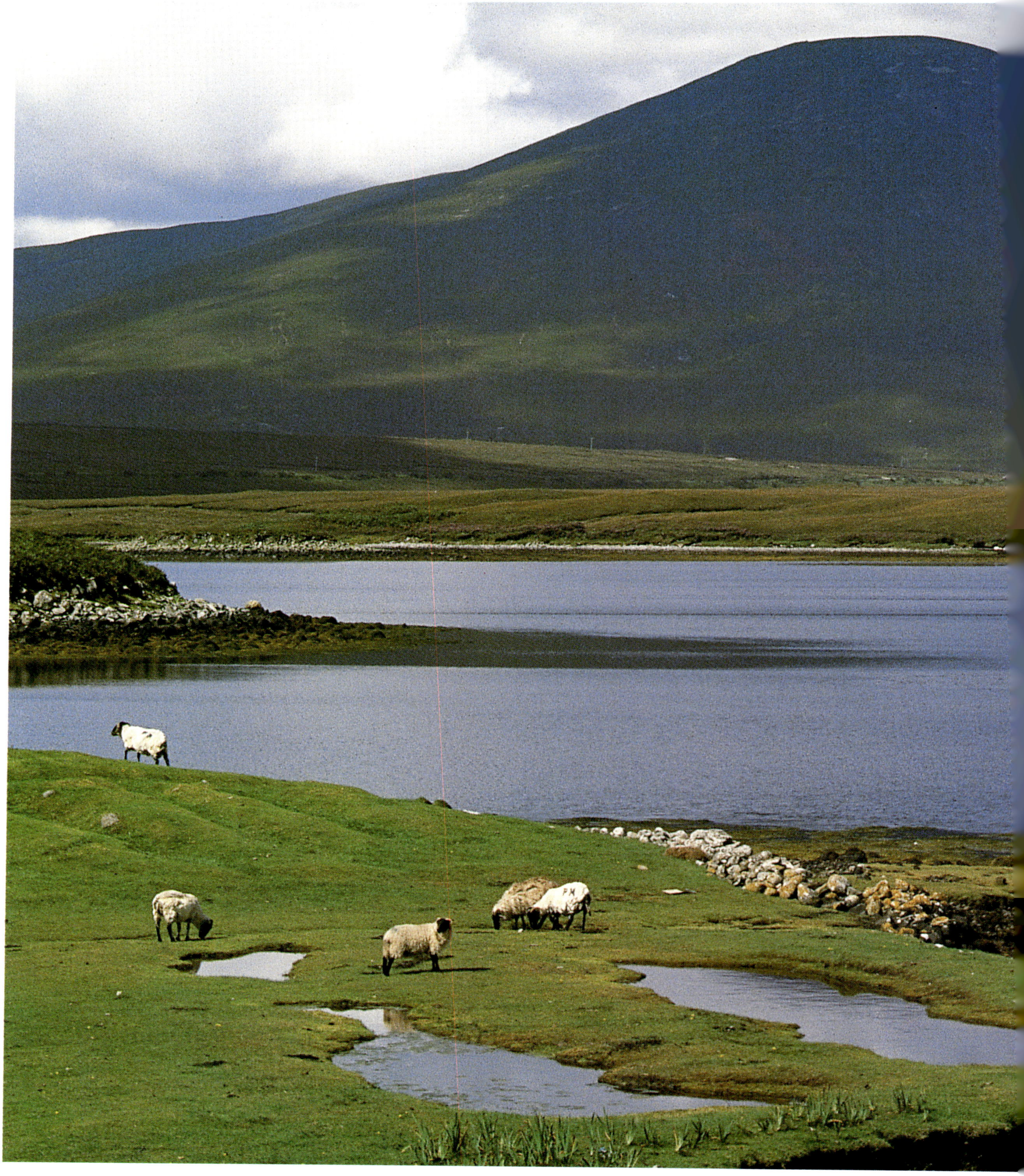

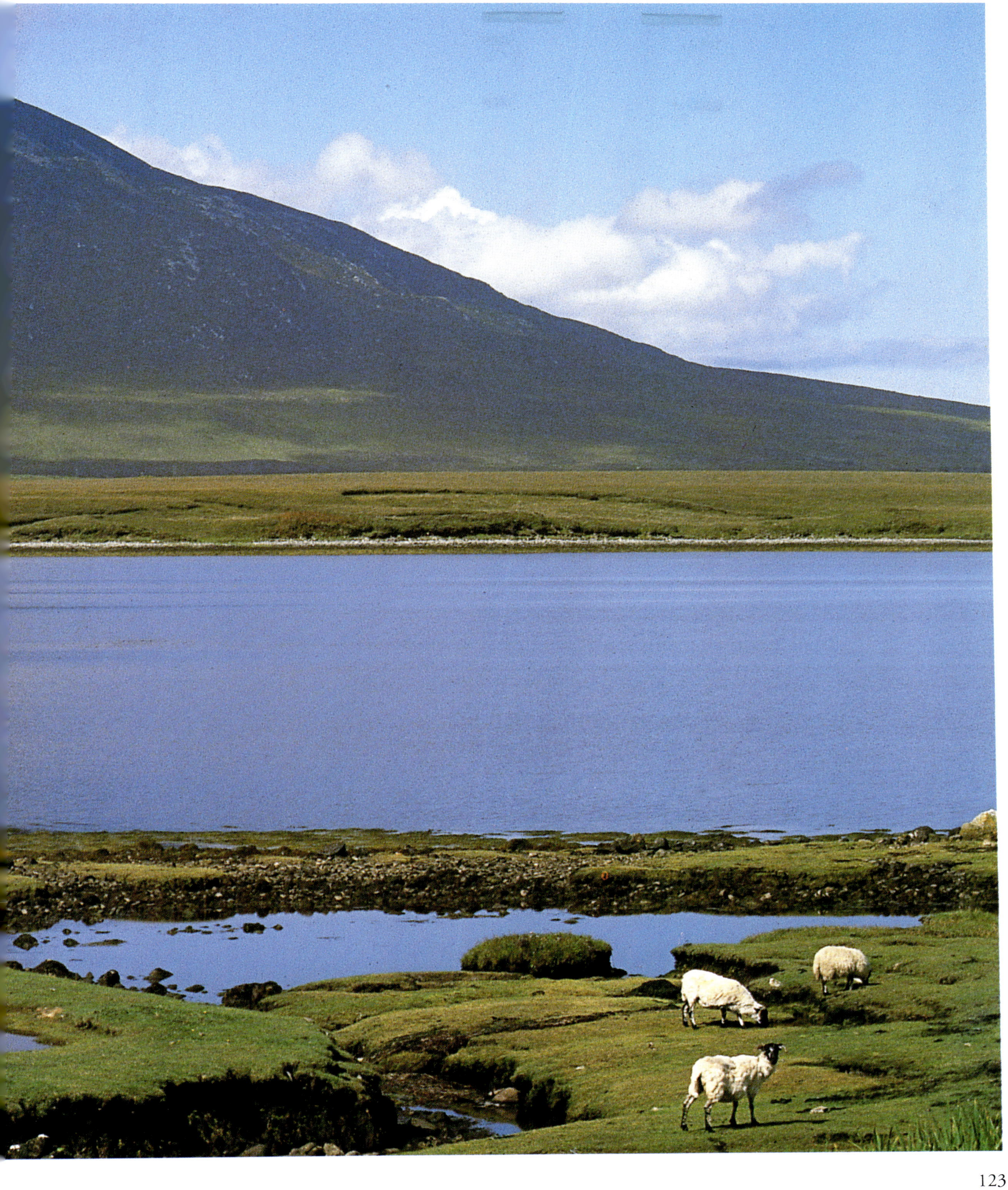

Achill Island impresses with its stark but beautiful landscapes.

Routes through Ireland - six suggestions

Circled figures refer to the route number in the map, see page 127

It is a matter of experiencing a landscape full of impressive natural beauty, and constantly changing bright colours. Whether on a bicycle or by car, you can get to know the interior of the island in comfort, and with absolutely no rush. Driving on the left is no problem either. The Irish are considerate drivers. Always give way to the other driver on the narrow roads, and remember to treat the oncoming driver in the same friendly way that he will treat you. The routes we have chosen are only recommendations, so we have kept these notes very brief. All the journeys are one day's touring. Most of the signposts are bilingual - in both English and Gaelic. In Donegal, Mayo, or Connemara you often find street signs in Gaelic only, with distances shown in miles. Most maps of Ireland are bilingual as well. We have found Michelin Map No. 405, on scale 1:400 000, very useful.

Route ①: From Dublin into the heart of the island

Dublin - Bray - Enniskerry - Glendalough - Kildare - Tullamore - Athlone - Roscommon - Castlepollard - Trim - Newgrange - Drogheda - Malahide - Howth (300 miles).

The starting point is Dublin. This is where the round trip south begins. A coastline can hardly offer a more romantic atmosphere than the one between Dun Laoghaire (James Joyce Tower) and Shankill. Beyond the resort of Bray is the mountain village of Enniskerry, surrounded by dense leafy woodland, and one of the most magnificent estates in Ireland: Powerscourt House and park (open to the public). The entrance gate originates from Germany's Bamberg cathedral, and the old railings come from a German castle. The main house was built in 1730, was burned down in 1975, and rebuilt again. The English park is a classic example of a vast garden landscape. Vast, interconnected woodlands, pastures and moors are typical of County Wicklow. Narrow, hilly roads lead into the valley of Glendalough (see p. 151), where the stone remains of one of the oldest monastery foundations in Europe can still be seen. The road winds through the Wicklow mountains to Hollywood, and through the green countryside on to Kildare, which is where the Irish horse stud farms are centred. The Japanese Garden close by (laid out between 1906 and 1910 by Japanese gardeners, and quite unique in the world) symbolises the human life cycle, using plants. The monastery ruin of Grey Abbey, dating from 1206, should not be missed. On the main road, the R 420, you carry on through the central Irish plain. Just before Tullamore the road goes over the Grand Canal - once an important waterway between Dublin and the Shannon. In Tullamore they make the well-known spirit "Irish Mist". Via Clara and Moate you come to Athlone, which is a water sports centre on the Shannon. Once the market square was of strategic importance: in the thirteenth century the first town wall was built and the foundation stone for the fortress, Athlone Castle, was laid. The building now houses a museum. The town was the site of the battles during the Williamite War (1689-91). To the north of Athlone is Lough Ree, with its dozen or so islands - a paradise for water sports enthusiasts and anglers. The croaking of frogs on the lakeside can be heard everywhere. There is a thirteenth century Dominican abbey on a hill at the edge of Roscommon. Even more interesting though is Clonalis House in Castlerea, a nineteenth-century manor house. The Clonalis Museum keeps the memory of the O'Connor clan alive.

Moorland and pasture landscapes, broken up by drumlin hills, and countless lakes and rivers are the predominant characteristics of the countryside around Longford, the chief town of the county of the same name. Through this fertile landscape, formerly woodland densely covered with oaks, you come to the N4 road, which branches at the Downs, towards Trim, the first Norman settlement. Part of the wall, which was 1500 feet or so long, and the fortress tower of Trim castle, built in 1172 and at one time the largest Norman castle and considered impregnable, have remained intact. Between Trim and Navan is the line of hills, including the Hill of Tara (see p. 154). The former residence of the chieftains of Meath was for 2,500 years, from about 2000 B.C. to 500 A.D., the centre of power on the whole island. The coronation stone, "Lia Fail" on the hill, is a reminder of that period of greatness for the Irish. A great convention was then held there every three years, the "Feis Teamhair", attended by nobles, druids, poets and warriors who came from all over the land. There are signboards which show how life must have been here 2,000 years ago. A monument of a quite different sort in the land of "gods and heroes" is Newgrange (see p. 154); it is a burial ground which is probably more than 4,000 years old. At this tourist attraction today, it does not require a great deal of imagination to realise what the magical effect of the stones must have been like on people then. The next town on the route, the trading town of Drogheda founded by the Vikings in 911, was often the scene of bloody conflict; in Cromwell's time the place was destroyed. Continuing on the N1 you reach Malahide and Howth harbour. This picturesque little town with Howth Castle, dating from 1654, lies on a peninsula to the north of Dublin. From 170 metres up, in the castle grounds, you can see Ireland's largest city and the peaks of the Mountains of Mourne. In May, when the rhododendrons bloom, Howth is at its best. The clean air is a remedy for asthma and bronchitis sufferers. Well-known Irish folk bands can be seen in the Abbey Tavern during the summer season.

Route ②: Through the wilds of Connemara to the mountains of Mayo

Galway - Cashel Bay - Clifden - Leenane - Westport - Keel - Bangor - Ballycastle - Ballina - Castlebar - Cong - Oughterard - Galway (230 miles).

No other landscape is as popular as Connemara. It is no surprise that activity on the roads there is somewhat livelier

Kylemore Abbey, which is not far from Letterfrack on the edge of a lake, seems more like a castle. A prosperous businessman built this for himself as a country home in the nineteenth century. Today there is a boarding school for young ladies, run by Benedictine nuns.

than in the rest of Ireland. The most beautiful approach to Connemara runs from busy Galway (see p. 150) along the R 336 to Casla. And there, at the crossroads, you must decide whether you want to discover a little more of the islands, in which case you go left to Lettermore, or whether to carry straight on towards Clifden. Certainly anyone who has the time should go for the diversionary trip, as the narrow roads through Lettermore and Gorumna Island are especially charming: scattered white cottages with their blue or red window frames make their mark on this stony, sparse land. The colours change as though in a kaleidoscope - brown, green, blue, grey to off-white. The magic of the light outdoes what can be seen from pictures. On the road to Clifden then, the countryside is marked by valleys covered in pine forest, lakes and fine sandy bays in which calves freely romp around. Clifden (see p. 145) is a brightly coloured tourist resort. Young people in particular love to come here - not least because of the excellent beaches.

On the main road of this approximately 230-mile long round trip, going towards Leenane, the romantic Kylemore Abbey lies hidden behind rhododendron bushes. It is a boarding school for young ladies, with souvenir shops and a tea room. The road along the steep Killary Harbour Bay, where they breed salmon, leads up hill and down dale. It runs past deep green hills, tobacco-brown peat bogs; the 2400 feet high Croagh Patrick (see p. 146), the holy mountain of the Irish, which is off to the left on the journey to Westport (see p. 154), a sea fishing centre. The N 59 leads to Mulrany and from there it joins the R 319 to Achill Island (see p. 131), and on to Keel. When you come back from the island it carries on to the N 59 through the wild Mayo district, via Bangor to Crossmolina. The wind constantly howls there over the moors and across the brown wilderness. Decayed houses and dead trees mark out the road. Around a tumbledown cottage, you can just make out furrows in the ground. Maybe the former inhabitants were farmers who, in 1846, emigrated to America during the dreadful famine.

Behind Ballycastle the road leads to the Atlantic coast. Above the cliffs of Downpatrick Head, where the waves of the Atlantic thunder against the rocks, there is a rainbow. A magnificent sight is the bay, where French troops landed in 1798 to support the Irish in their battle for freedom against the English, at Killala. Not far from there is the famous Moyne Abbey. That too is now a ruin.

Ballina, (see p. 133) on the river Moy with its teeming fish, is a lively market centre. In the fish smoking factory on the main road, exquisite salmon is for sale. Along the R 310 you come to Castlebar, the chief town of County Mayo. Mayo is one of the most sparsely populated parts of the Republic, and neither have the tourists yet discovered this barren landscape for themselves. Cyclists dreaming of freedom and independence come here to pedal the empty roads. To the south of Castlebar is the vast river and lakeland country of Lough Mask. Then there is flat pasture land again, closed in by three-foot-high stone walls, which are so typical in Ireland. Back on the N 59, you come to the holiday resort of Oughterard, and from there a narrow and lonely mountain road leads to Casla. From here now, it is not very far back to our starting point.

Route ③: Ireland in miniature
Kinvarra - Ballyvaughan - Burren - Cliffs of Moher - Lahinch - Kilkee - Kilrush - Ennis (160 miles).

This round trip runs through countryside which could not be found more varied anywhere. It is Ireland in miniature, so to speak. Pasture land changes into the grey of the limestone region, The Burren, where the Cliffs of Moher, over 600 feet high, form a delightful contrast to the beautiful countryside around Corofin. This is the region for coastal anglers, cyclists, hikers, bird watchers, and botanists from all over the world. The journey begins in Kinvarra. The colourful little harbour here is an absolute must for photographers. Along the coast, past a few castles, you come to the fishing village of Ballyvaughan. Monk's Pub in the port is a favourite meeting point. The road winds up from the village on to the karst landscape of The Burren (see page 136), with the Poulnabrone Dolmen, Ireland's best known Stone Age burial ground.

Along the coast the road leads to the Cliffs of Moher (see p. 145), which are about 800 feet high. One has the most splendid view from O'Brien's Tower. The best known bathing resort is Lahinch, which with its white houses, its beautiful beach and golf course, gives the impression of being extremely well heeled. Favourite areas for walking are Freagh and Spanish Point, so called because six ships of the Spanish Armada sank there in 1588. Kilkee is also gaining ground as a bathing resort. The R 473 goes past Kilrush to the Mouth of Shannon estuary and on to Ennis (see p. 150).

Route ④: On the way to the westernmost point in Europe
Limerick - Tarbert - Tralee - Dingle - Killorglin - Waterville - Killarney - Macroom - Kinsale (420 kilometres).

On this journey you will become acquainted with a countryside rich in variety: large lakes, breathtakingly sheer coastlines, and inviting beaches. The stretch from Limerick through Tarbert and Tralee goes along the well-built N 69 to the Dingle peninsula (see p. 147), where the Gaelic language and culture are still strongly preserved. The route winds over the plain and then up to the Connor Pass, which is about 1500 feet up. The view from here - underneath the 200 feet high Slievnae - is breathtakingly beautiful. When you reach Slea Head you are at the westernmost tip of Europe. There are a few stone, beehive-shaped huts. These "beehive huts" were once lived in by monks. The road goes through Ventry to Dingle, and from there on to Killorglin. Beyond the town, on the N 70, begins the Ring of Kerry, which is one of Ireland's most popular destinations for an outing. You get an absolutely overpowering impression of the Atlantic Ocean here. Then comes Cahirciveen, the birthplace of Ireland's champion of freedom, Daniel O'Connell, and beyond that Waterville. 8 miles away to the west from the Coomakistapas can be seen the 700-foot high Skellig islands; Irish monks once lived there in complete solitude. Nowadays one of Europe's largest colonies of gannets lives on the island. Near Castlecove a small road turns off from the N 70 and leads to Staigue Stone Fort, a ring fort which is about 2500 years old. Parknasilla invites you to wander through what seems like a sub-tropical landscape, along the coast as far as Blackwater Bridge. Between Kenmare and Killarney the road leads through a particularly beautiful area of Ireland's woodland and lakes. Killarney, on the edge of the National Park of the same name, attracts huge numbers of tourists all the year round. It is the epicentre of Irish tourism, the single most celebrated beauty spot in all of Ireland.

Route ⑤: Along the coast of Northern Ireland
Belfast - Larne - Ballycastle - Giant's Causeway - Portrush - Coleraine - Derry (120 kilometres).

The A 2 is undoubtedly among the most impressive of coast roads, running as it does between Belfast (see p. 135)

Dingle (top), Ballyvaughan (centre), and Kinvara (bottom) are among Ireland's west coast destinations, in which Gaelic is still the main language spoken by the local people, and Gaelic traditions are particularly well maintained.

One of the most imposing examples of military architecture in medieval Ireland is the ponderous King John's Castle in Limerick, built in the thirteenth century.

Top left: In Cahirciveen, where the legendary Irish patriot and freedom fighter Daniel O'Connell (1775 - 1847) was born.

Bottom left: Romanesque church in Kilmalkedar on the Dingle peninsula, with an alphabet stone which should be visited. The shapes of the building were adopted from Cormac's Chapel in Cashel.

Right: View across the Shannon at Limerick.

and Derry, almost entirely along the Atlantic Coast. You leave Belfast in the direction of Carrickfergus, once the most important port in Northern Ireland, and with the best preserved castle on the whole island, dating from the twelfth century. After Larne comes the splendid Antrim coast, extending through Ballycastle (see p. 135) to Portrush. This craggy coastline, with its shining red and white cliffs, always offers impressive, and sometimes breathtaking views. The ruin of Dunluce Castle, built by the Earl of Ulster, is worth visiting, and there is the Giant's Causeway, the world famous natural monument, which is under United Nations protection. The coastal road ends at the resort of Portrush. Finally the journey carries on through Coleraine to its destination of Derry (see p. 147).

Route ⑥: A journey through Donegal, the lonely, wild North West.

Donegal - Killybegs - Glen Bay - Ardara - Port Noo - Bloody Foreland - Glenveagh - National Park - Milford - Fanad Peninsula - Ramelton - Letterkenny - Buncrana - Malin Head - Moville - Grianan of Aileach (160 miles).

The Province of Donegal, forming a border with Northern Ireland, is only linked to the Republic by a narrow tongue of land. This most remote and most lonely area of Ireland can still be regarded as a well-kept secret. Only one access road leads from the Republic into the land of myths, hills and lakes, and that is the N 15, which goes over the bridge at Ballyshannon and on to the town of Donegal (see p. 147). This route, which is about 160 miles long, starts in Donegal, and its first destination is the fishing village of Killybegs on the N 56. Sea-anglers set out from there for the sea. Then comes the particularly varied road to Glencolumbkille, where the Folk Village is worth a visit. From here, there is a splendid view over the Atlantic from Glen Bay and Glen Head. The walk from the Slieve League cliffs is also particularly impressive, and you can climb them from Carrick. The road to Ardara winds through a mountain landscape, well-known for its tweed woven products and the Holy Family Black Church. Fog often hangs over and in front of the indented coastline, reinforcing the impression of wild romance. Bloody Foreland was so named because of the rust-red cliffs which shine a fiery red at sunset. On the mighty cliffs of Horn Head, about 600 feet high, wind and water have carved their own strange shapes into the Marble Arch. Offshore are the islands of Inishbofin and Tory Island. Creeslough with its 2000-foot high Muckish Mountain is the starting point for walks through the Ards Forest. The Glenveagh National Park stretches between the R 251 and Letterkenny. In this area of 6 square miles or so, is a castle which is a possible starting point for several walks. Doe Castle is the ancestral seat of the once mighty MacSweeny clan. North of Milford is the mountainous Fanad peninsula, through which the scenic route runs for about 40 miles: countless inlets, gorges, mountains and bizarre rock formations make up the landscape here. In Rathmullen, on the banks of Lough Swilly, are the ruins of a fifteenth century Cistercian monastery, and in Rathmelton a few Georgian houses bear witness to the former prosperity of

Far to the North, a Creeslough in County Donegal, is the ruin of Doe Castle on a peninsula. This sixteenth century castle is a national monument.

This church with its traditional round tower is in Donegal, in the lovely north west of the island.

those who ran the cloth weaving industry. Where the river Swilly disgorges into Lough Swilly is the most important town in County Donegal, Letterkenny. The N 13 leads from there to the Inishowen peninsula. Taking the coastal route to Carndonagh, you pass through Buncrana and Ballyliffen, and drive past inviting beaches. On the way to the most northerly point in Ireland, Malin Head, you pass by the oldest Relief Cross on the island, the seventh century Donagh Cross, at about 3 km inland from Carndonagh. The R 238 leads over the lonely moorland, heathland and meadow landscape to Lough Foyle, which separates Northern Ireland from the Republic at this point. In Greencastle, opposite Magilligan Point and on the narrowest point of the fjord, Richard de Burgh built a castle as far back as 1305, and in 1812 the place was given a fort. Following the coastal road, you come to Muff. From there, the road carries on to Grianan of Aileach, a prehistoric hill-fort. The fifteen-foot high walls extend over a length of 230 feet. This was built about 3,700 years ago. The structure was restored between 1874 and 1878. The "Sun Palace" is supposed to have been known to Ptolemy of Alexandria (about 200 B.C.). Finally, the N 13, N 56 and N 15 take you back to the starting point in Donegal.

A to Z of tourist attractions and landscapes

Figures in circles refer to the map on page 155. Letters inside circles refer to the Dublin street map on page 148.

Achill Island ①. There has been a bridge over Achill Sound since 1888. There is therefore a land connection from this 100 sq. miles Irish island to the Corraun peninsula and the rest of the world. The Atlantic Drive, which runs along the sheer cliff coastline of the island to Dooega, offers views to make you dizzy. Worth a visit are the old churchyard and the fifteenth-century *Killdownet Tower*, the remains of what was formerly the fortress of the legendary "pirate queen", Grace O'Malley, who as a nineteen-year-old inherited it from her father, and because of her successful raids, had become a threat to the English rulers. Queen Elizabeth I put a price on her head, but the English laid siege to her fortress in vain. During an audience with Elizabeth I Grace, who politely refused the title of countess which was offered to her, was treated as a lady of equal status. The conquest of Ireland began under the Tudors, in particular Henry VIII (1491 - 1547) and Elizabeth I (1533 - 1603), and was successfully completed under William III in 1691. The later counts of Mayo are thought to be Grace's descendants. Her name has survived in song and story, and there has even been a new biography of her in recent years.

The *Cathedral Rocks* are a special attraction, with their

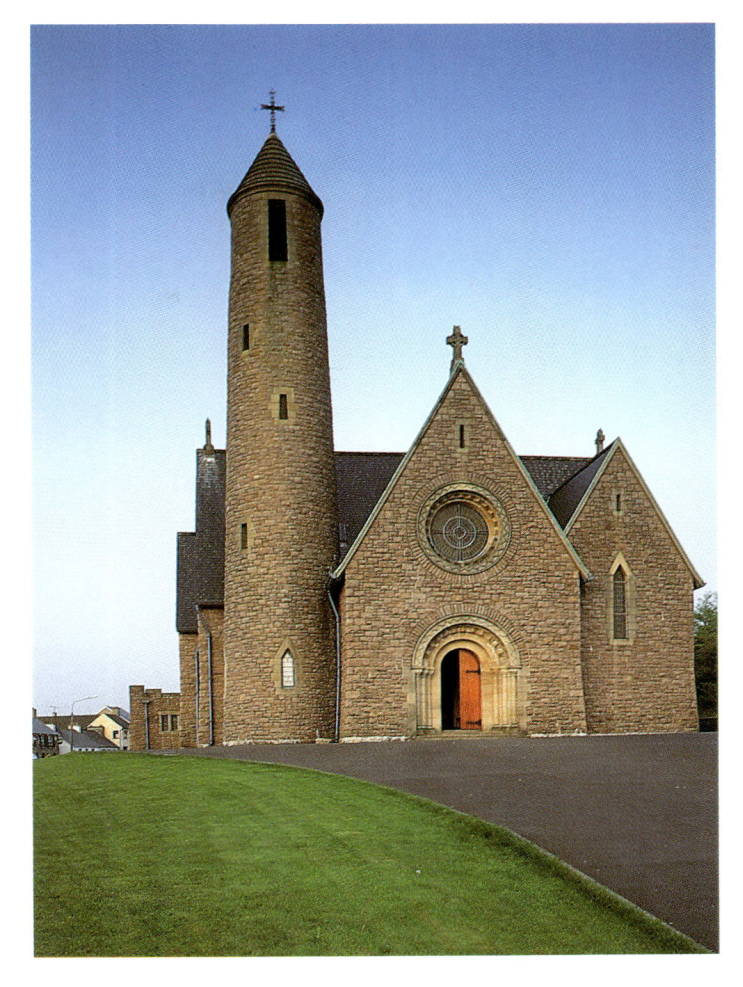

Every year on St. Columba's Day, the 9th June, a pilgrimage takes place at Glencolumbkille in honour of the saint after whom the place is named. The individual stations are marked by patterned sandstones, decorated with cross motifs and rigorous geometrical patterns.

grottoes and sheer cliff face. From there Clare Island can be seen to the South. Large numbers of common seal and dolphins can be seen swimming along its coastline. This is also where rainbows occur most frequently in Ireland.

There is an impressive stretch of sheer coastline between Achill Head and Keel, which looks as though cut by a razor-sharp knife. Keel has a large sandy beach which is wonderful for romantic walks. You can also go by boat from there across to the *Seal Caves*. There are prehistoric burial grounds to be found at Slievemore as well. Not least, Achill Island was well known to the German author Heinrich Böll, who owned a cottage in the village of Dugort into the 1970s, and while there wrote his world-famous *Irish Diary*. Nowadays the island's inhabitants make a living mainly from fishing, sheep-rearing and tourism.

Adare ②. With its thatched houses, this rates as one of Ireland's prettiest villages. It lies about 16 km south west of Limerick, on the Maigue river, which is well-known for its abundance of fish (salmon and trout). In this village of fewer than a thousand inhabitants, the wonderfully preserved ruins of the *Franciscan Abbey*, dating from 1464, and the thirteenth century *Desmond Castle* are to be admired, and the fourteenth-century bridge, with its 14 stone arches. Today *Adare Manor*, built in Tudor neo-Gothic style in 1832, houses an interesting collection of paintings. Also in a very good state of preservation are the main nave, choir and one aisle of the Augustine monastery founded in 1325.

Aran Islands ③. The three bare limestone islands of Inishmore, Inishmaan and Inisheer are about 50 km to the west of Galway, opposite the foothills of Galway Bay. Geologically speaking, the Aran islands are a continuation of the Burren karst landscape, and in the summer months there is greenery and flowers between the limestone deposits. These three islands were inhabited as far back as the Stone Age. A good 1,400 inhabitants of this group of islands speak Gaelic, and maintain the old Irish culture. It is the only place in Ireland where some kind of folk costume has evolved. These islands are therefore a real treasure chest for antiquarian researchers, linguists and folklorists in their various investigations, though the writer Tim Robinson warns: "The boats don't go out there any more [...] so you will understand, that we cannot be compared with people in the towns or in the mild plains. ..... There just won't be any more people like us."

Several church ruins are among the attractions, including the eighth-century Teampall Breachain, and the stone fortification *Dún Aenghus*, which stands on the 270-foot high sheer cliffs of Kilmurrey, on Inishmore. The ring-wall fortress consists of three concentric semi-circles, the middle one of which is about 150 feet in diameter. This building is one of the best preserved stone age forts in Europe. Inishmore is also the largest of the islands, with its 14 villages, in which a total of about 900 people live. The ruin of *Arkyne's Castle* in Killeany is a

Top left: The environment around Ballina, County Mayo spreads a highly individual, melancholy atmosphere. The road runs through a monotonous moorland landscape for mile upon mile.

The greater part of Achill Island is covered by heath and moorland. Only here and there do small villages, donkeys, cows or small fishing boats act as a reminder that human life is present in this bare landscape (bottom left, centre, and right).

reminder of Cromwell's propensity for drastic action: for that building apparently, four churches and a round tower were all pulled down.

The Dublin born dramatist John Millington Synge (1871 - 1909), who wrote *Riders to the Sea*, lived on Inishmaan, the second largest island. In 1934 the documentary film directed by Robert Flaherty, under the title of *Man of Aran*, was highly successful. The stone ring-fort of *Dún Conor*, built in an oval shape with 20 foot high walls is excellently preserved, and most impressive. Also worth visiting is an old house of prayer from the Early Christian era, the *Church of the Canons*. On Inisheer, the smallest of the islands, there are no cars on the narrow roads, and ponies or donkeys are the main means of transport.

Armagh ④. This town, first mentioned in 289 B.C., has about 13,000 inhabitants and is one of Ireland's main religious centres. It is the see of both the Catholic and the Anglican archbishops. The cathedrals for both faiths are landmarks facing each other on two hills. Both are dedicated to St. Patrick. The Protestant *St. Patrick's Cathedral* is today on the precise spot where the saint founded his first church in 443. The present building, which was begun in the twelfth century, is of English late Gothic style, and very much changed in the nineteenth century. The crypts, however, go back to the tenth century. The Catholic church of the same name (built between 1840 and 1904) is most impressive with its 200-foot high double towers. The *Observatory* built back in 1791 and the only *Planetarium* in Northern Ireland have now been brought together in the Astronomy Centre. The *Public Library* (founded in 1781) houses one of the most important collections of early manuscripts and historical works in Ireland. The countryside around Armagh is also called the "Garden of Ulster" because of its many fruit plantations.

Ballina ⑤. There is something melancholy about the drive through the highlands of the Ox Mountains. The hills are either bare or covered with monotonous fir plantations, and the wind whips through the valleys. Ballina on the other hand, situated on the River Moy and a good starting point for angling parties on Lough Cullin, or Lough Conn with its teeming fish, and indeed for journeys into the mountains of County Mayo, gives an impression of life and bustle. There is a sixth-century dolmen not far from the railway station; it is the grave of four brothers who supposedly murdered their foster father. At the mouth of the river, in the wide Killala Bay, are the well-preserved cloister buildings of *Rosserk Friary* (founded about 1440) and *Moyne Abbey* (1460). The French Revolutionary Army, which the Irish wanted to support during their struggle for freedom against the English, landed in the bay on 22 August 1798. After early successes though, they were beaten off by the English. French troops had tried to land in Bantry Bay two years earlier, but a devastating storm ruined that enterprise.

IN THE LAND OF BETTING AND RACING FANATICS

The two men were called Blake and O'Callaghan and in 1752 they challenged each other to a horse race which resulted in a new world entering the English language: steeplechase. These Anglo-Irish gentlemen ran a race about 4 miles across open country, and over ditches and stone walls. They were aiming for the church steeple in the village of St. Leger, near Doneraile. Subsequently, all races over solid jumps and ditches have been called steeplechases.

Point-to-point races are very popular in the country, where they are village events with no race course. They go over fields and meadows, walls and fallen tree trunks. These events mostly take place in the winter months, and there are wild goings-on with it; the beer flows liberally, and there is no shortage of bookmakers, who, standing on a bench or bales of straw, encourage people in loud voices to place a bet.

A much more genteel public meets at the famous race meetings at the Curragh in Co. Kildare, about 30 miles south of Dublin in the heartland of Irish stud farming. It is the headquarters of Irish racing: the Irish classics are run here. Ireland has 31 race courses, on which about 180 races are run every year. The Dublin Horse Show, in the Ballsbridge district of the city, which since 1868 has always been held in the first week in August, is a social occasion, but at the same time it is also a point of transfer for all thoroughbreds and other horses from all over the country. Ireland breeds more race horses and ponies than any other European country. The horses are regarded as having natural talent, bred as they are in this mild island climate in green meadows, looked after by experienced trainers and ridden by the best jockeys in the world. Dealers from England and America, from Germany, France and the Arab Emirates meet each other at this horse show. There are also important horse markets held in Dingle, Limerick and Ballinasloe. The annual turnover in thoroughbreds is estimated at around 44 million pounds.

There is a horse race held somewhere in the country almost every day, and the daily papers devote a lot of space to the sport. Of course, there is much at stake on the outcome of the race. The real fanatics in all this will not be found on the race course, but in the nearby pubs or betting shops, where they follow the race on television, sweating and shouting, to see who has won.

Riding as a sport for its own sake reaches its high point in winter with fox hunting. Each county has its own hunting club, which, however, is always led by a rich landowner, who can afford his own pack of hounds. These clubs, which call themselves such names as the "Galway Blazers" or the "Black and Tans" have already lost some of their exclusivity: anyone who can ride and can afford to pay the subscription fee can join in.

There are constant protests against the cruel pursuit of the foxes, and indeed against hare coursing, in which two greyhounds pursue a live hare, whose only chance of survival is to escape through the hole in the fence at the end of the race track.

Greyhound races are a bit more "progressive", however, in which a pack of greyhounds chase after an electrically operated "hare". Here too, everything is drowned out by the racing reports coming over the loudspeaker, and the incitement of spectators to action, coming from the bookmakers in their hoarse voices, encouraging visitors to place their bet.

The select, well-dressed public at the Horse Races in Dublin, or Kildare.

Village races reach a wider public; they are held in an available meadow.

In Bunratty Folk Park over 20 houses from the counties of Clare, Limerick, and Tipperary have been restored to their original condition. They provide an interesting insight into country lifestyle, working conditions and housing in the past.

Wolfe Tone, the spiritual leader of the fight for freedom and a supporter of the French Revolution, was captured by the English and committed suicide in prison rather than let his captors hang him.

Ballycastle ⑥. This Northern Irish town is a suitable stopping place on the journey from Larne to Portrush, along the Antrim Coast Road. Just offshore is *Rathlin Island*, which is home to about 100 people, ten times as many sheep, and 175 different types of birds. The parish has a population of about 4000, and among its attractions are a church built in 1756, and a few houses from the early nineteenth century. A narrow path leads to the 600-foot high, precipitous basalt columns of *Fair Head*, which further west become the extraordinary natural wonder which is the *Giant's Causeway* (see p. 150).

Bantry ⑦. Bantry is in the bay of the same name in the south west of the island, against the impressive backdrop of the Caha Mountains. Offshore on the western side, *Whiddy Island* shields Bantry Harbour from the sea. Because of the moderating effect of the Gulf Stream on the climate, even fuchsia hedges and palms thrive here.

Bantry House is on the outskirts of town in a magnificent park. This Georgian-style manor house contains a unique collection of tapestries, furniture and porcelain, and gives a wonderful insight into the former lifestyle of the nobility.

Belfast ⑧. Belfast had a fort as long ago as the early Middle Ages, which was destroyed in 1177. For centuries, it was a small port; later, it was important as a linen town. It now has about half a million inhabitants and is the provincial capital of Ulster (Northern Ireland), a university town and the most important industrial town in the North. In 1912 the Harland & Wolff shipyard on Queen's Island built what was then the largest passenger liner in the world, and considered unsinkable - the "Titanic".

Belfast has made many headlines because of the numerous terrorist attacks. If you want to get from the largest Catholic residential area in the Falls Road into what is probably the best known Protestant area of Shankill Road, then you must for security reasons make a detour through the city centre. In the city centre and University area, you are on neutral ground. This is also where the city centre tourist attractions are. Not to be missed is the towering *City Hall* (1906) - an imposing dome-shaped building in Renaissance style, and this is the central point. Nearby is the Protestant *St. Anne's Cathedral*, begun in 1899 and finished only a few years ago, with its three remarkable west portals and in the baptismal chapel a mosaic floor made of hundreds of thousands of miniature glass beads. The *Albert Memorial Clock Tower,* built in 1869 in memory of Prince Albert, Queen Victoria's consort, called by local people the "Big Ben of Belfast" because of its similarity to its London counterpart. The city is justly proud of its *Botanical Gardens*, in which the 135-year-old palm house and the tropical gorge are the outstanding attractions. Among other things in the Ulster Museum, finds from the Celtic and Early Christian period are on display; also noteworthy is the gold and silver treasure from the galleon "Girona", which along with other ships in the Spanish Armada, perished in 1588, in the storm off the coast of Antrim. *Queen's University* was built in Tudor style, between 1845 and 1894; it has been independent since 1909, and also houses the Historical Museum. Approximately three miles to the east of the city is a symbol of Unionist dominance and power: the Palladian style Parliament building, or Stormont, built between 1928 and 1932. It was the official residence of the Prime Minister and the meeting place for the Northern Ireland Parliament, which was abolished in 1972.

Boyle ⑨. To the south west of Lough Key, at the foot of the Curlew Hills, lies the market town of Boyle, on the river of the same name. This was the birthplace of Edward King, who provided the historical model for the moving lamentation by John Milton (1608-1674) of "Lycidas". The transition from Romanesque to the Gothic style of architecture can be seen particularly well from what is left of the well-preserved ruins of the Cistercian establishment of *Boyle Abbey* (founded 1161).

Bunratty Castle ⑩. Not far from Shannon airport is Ireland's only remaining wholly preserved fortress. This fortress, dating from 1467, was in the hands of the O'Briens, Counts of Thomand, in the sixteenth and seventeenth centuries. What is probably the most authentic example of a medieval castle was lived in until into the nineteenth century, and was restored in 1960 and fitted out with furniture and paintings from the fifteenth and sixteenth centuries. Nowadays, on summer evenings, the castle is the busy scene of "medieval banquets". On the castle estate a museum of local history and culture was established as *Bunratty Folk Park*, with typical country cottages and Irish farmhouses, which have been transplanted here from all over the country. Over 20 buildings from the counties of Clare, Limerick and Tipperary were rebuilt for this purpose. Next to the castle tower is the old pub "Dirty Nelly's" dating from 1620, in which folk music is played, and freshly caught salmon from the river Shannon are on the menu.

Burren ⑪. The lonely, 170 square mile plateau of The Burren, on the south side of Galway Bay, is in its bare ruggedness a wildly romantic area, and for its type is quite unparalleled anywhere in Europe. *Boireann* as it is called in Old Gaelic, meaning stony ground, is a unique karst landscape, a tableland rising in flat steps, made up from unfolded layers of limestone. One can get some idea here, of what Europe might have looked like at the end of the last Ice Age, when the glaciers had melted and left a whole lot of boulders behind. In between the 270 million or so

Only a few buildings in Belfast act as a reminder of the town's former elegance. In the eighteenth century it was described as "the Athens of the North". A few rows of houses still show traces of that time (top) ...
as also does St. Anne's Cathedral, built between 1899 and 1904, in Neo-romanesque style, and which is the headquarters of the Anglican Church of Ireland (centre). Extensive inner city areas of Belfast were destroyed during the unrest which was close to civil war conditions in Northern Ireland, or they have had to give way to modern glass and reinforced concrete structures (below).

Continuation page 145

Unaffected by the civil war conditions, which persisted in the country for years, the little Northern Irish harbour of Portbradden nestles under sheer cliffs.

At the southern end of the Strangford Lough lies the especially attractive settlement of the same name, which was founded by the Vikings. The strategic importance of the place is made clear enough by four sixteenth-century Anglo-Norman defensive structures in the immediate vicinity. Anyone for whom the mellow green of the meadows and the soft breeze is not refreshing enough ....

... can take a courageous plunge into the waters of the lake.

On the coast road between Ballycastle and Ballintoy in Northern Ireland, sheep quite often stop for a rest. However, well-practised drivers skilfully weave their way through these moving obstacles ....

.... and head for the Giant's Causeway. This major tourist attraction consists of upright basalt pillars, arranged in groups standing up to 80 feet high. The most impressive of these formations is referred to as the "amphitheatre".

Double page overleaf: Portrush on the Northern Irish coast. A stately row of Victorian houses faces the sea.

139

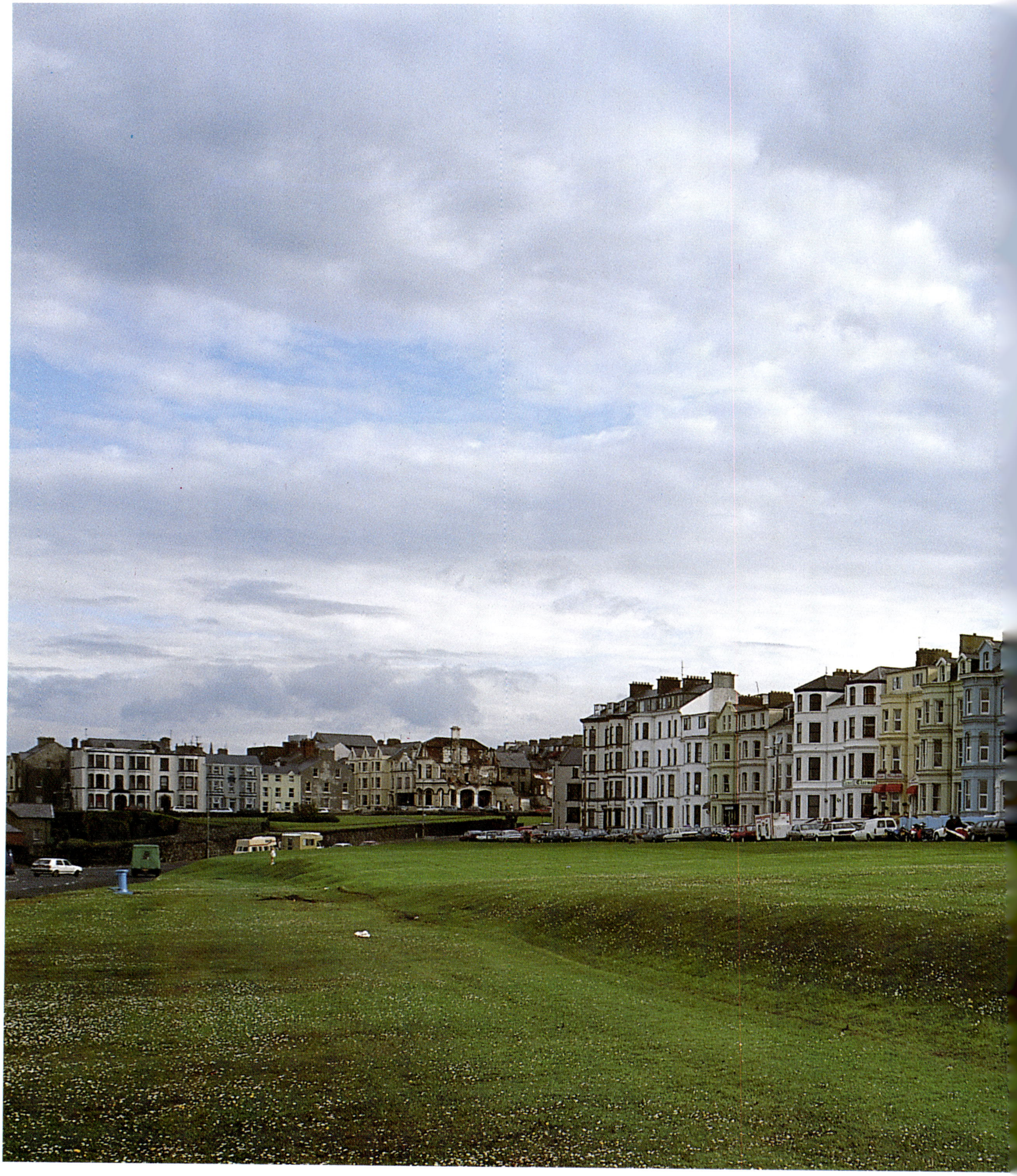

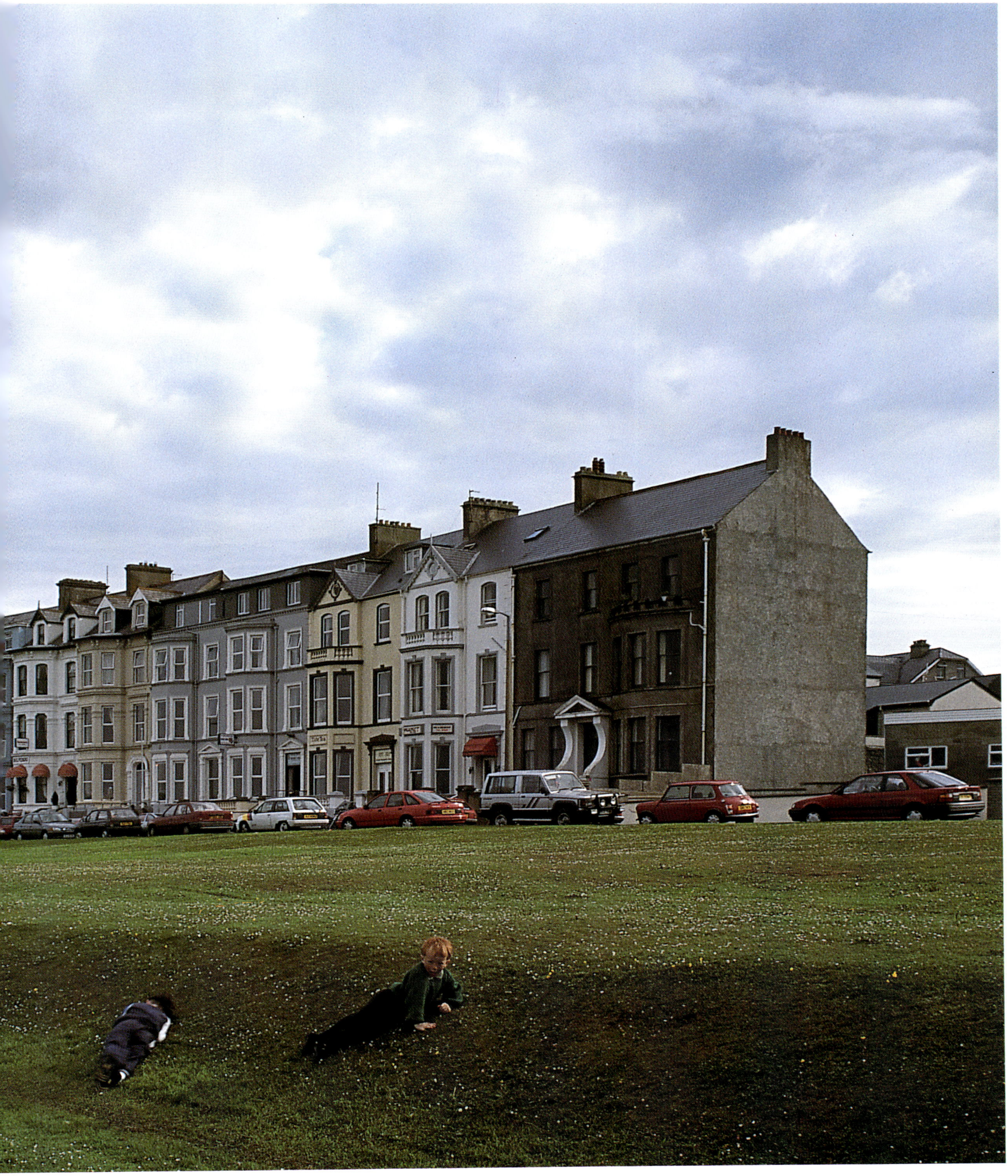

The Ulster Folk and Transport Museum, near Belfast, invites you to take an excursion into the past. Here you can stroll through little narrow lanes which have been rebuilt faithful to the originals, with the little shops ...

... or watch craftsmen at work, wearing costumes from the period. As this wax-drawing workshop shows, in the nineteenth century candles were hung up on a frame to dry out.

This lady is demonstrating, in one of the rebuilt Northern Irish farmhouses, how in the country people used to cook over an open fire ...

... and you can also visit a smithy of the period, with all the tools and accessories.

Dunluce Castle, on the Northern Irish coast, provides an enchanting view. This castle, which originates from the fourteenth century, stands on cliffs high above the sea, and is separated from the rest of the coastline by a deep moat, which is crossed over by only one small bridge.

year old, seemingly so bare, limestone blocks, under which there are subterranean lakes and rivers, caves and grottoes, an impressive range of flora reveals itself in the months from May to July: thistles, orchids, lady's slipper, maidenhair ferns dating from before the Ice Age, gentian, Irish saxifrage, and dozens of other species attract botanists and lovers of flowers from all over the world year by year, to study and gaze in amazement at that unique collection of Arctic, Mediterranean, and Alpine plants. Of the many caves in the area, *Aillwee Cave* near Ballyvaughan is open to visitors and easily accessible through its passages of up to 1000 feet. The Burren must have been inhabited long before the Christian era. A reminder of that are the old burial grounds, stone coffin graves and dolmens, stones raised up pointing skywards, which support a covering stone weighing several tons, lying across them as protection, so to speak. The dolmens are considered the simplest form of megalithic graves. The most famous one in The Burren is the restored *Poulnabrone Dolmen* on the road between Kilfenora and Ballyvaughan. The cover stone weighs 30 tons.

Particularly in the evening, or when it is raining, this high plateau has a mythical, unreal and enchanted feel about it.

In Kilfenora the *Burren Display Centre* tells you about the special features, the archaeology, geology, flora and fauna, and history of the development of this incomparable primeval landscape. To the east of the site is the ruin of *Kilfenora Cathedral* (twelfth century), of which the roofed western part is still in use. The open choir with its beautiful East Window incorporates likenesses of former bishops from the thirteenth and fourteenth centuries. Within the churchyard are three crosses, partly decorated with twelfth-century ornaments; there is another one outside, in a cattle meadow.

Carlow ⑫. This small town, with a population today of around 12,000 inhabitants, was once much disputed territory, because of its strategic position at the confluence of the Barrow with the river Burren. The Anglo-Normans fortified the place in 1361 for the first time with town walls. Several attacks, sieges and cases of arson are recorded up to 1650. During the rising of 1798, 640 rebellious Irishmen met their deaths here. They are remembered by a Celtic style monument. Of the once mighty *Carlow Castle* (thirteenth century) only the eastern side with two round towers at the corners has been preserved. The *Court House* built in 1830 in the classical style, with its Doric pillar gallery is an imitation of the Parthenon in Athens, and deserves a visit.

St. Patrick's College, a seminary for priests, was one of the first in Ireland, where teaching of the Catholic faith was officially permitted by the British rulers. Three kilometres to the east, there stands a 4,000-year-old dolmen, on the *Browne's Hill* land, and at one hundred tons, its cover stone is the heaviest in Ireland. One of the most impressive Celtic high crosses, the *Cross of Moone* (ninth century), is on the site of the former Franciscan abbey - eleven kilometres to the north east of the town.

Cashel ⑬. Tipperary's extremely hilly hinterland is absolutely full of ruins. There is one which stands out most strikingly from this productive farming land: the complex of buildings on the *Rock of Cashel*. There is a fortress which was the seat of the kings of Munster between 370 and 1101, on a limestone hill about 200 feet high. Then in the twelfth century they started with the church buildings - first of all the Romanesque *Cormac's Chapel* (1127–1134), and then later the Gothic cross-shaped *St. Patrick's Cathedral* (building started in 1169) - and Cashel became one of Ireland's most important religious centres. The Romanesque chapel has two towers and three entrances, and its well preserved frescoes with subjects from Greek mythology come as a surprise. A round tower from the thirteenth century and the fortress-like, restored accommodation tower of *Vicar's Choral Hall* (fifteenth century), in which there is a fifteenth-century high cross, are also well preserved. Just one kilometre to the west of the Rock of Cashel lie the eloquent ruins of *Hore Abbey*, founded by the Benedictines and taken over in 1272 by the Cistercians. Cashel itself can offer what is thought to be the first Dominican church in Ireland - with its thirteenth-century pointed arch windows - and an armoured tower house, the fifteenth-century *Quirke's Castle*. Today this is used as a hotel with a special historical charm.

Clifden ⑭. The flight from the land, which is obvious in so many villages in Connemara, has not yet afflicted Clifden. The beautiful location of this small market centre between the *Twelve Bens*, a chain of mountains to the east, and the indented Atlantic coastline, draws many tourists all the year round. They often include children, who want to see the beloved ponies of Connemara. To the south east of the town are hundreds of small lakes, in a vast moorland.

Cliffs of Moher ⑮. The Cliffs of Moher rise up almost perpendicular from the sea, to the south of Galway Bay. The natural phenomenon which occurs to the north west of Lahinch, near Liscannor, is particularly impressive during a storm. The sandstone cliffs, which rise up to 400 feet around *Hag's Head* to the south, and even 600 feet near *O'Brien's Tower* to the north, are linked to each other by an eight kilometre long, almost flat, plateau. In clear weather the view from O'Brien's Tower reaches as far as the *Aran Islands* (see p. 132). Thousands of birds, such as the brightly coloured puffins, guillemots, fulmars, and of course gulls, found in huge numbers here, nest among the cliffs.

Clonmacnoise ⑯. Of all historical ruins, the monastery founded in 545 by St. Ciaran is among the most impressive. On the "Island of Saints and Scholars", situated on the banks of the Shannon, are the remains of seven church ruins from various centuries, in what was once the largest monastic complex in Europe. In the centre is the tenth-century *Cathedral*, built in the Irish Romanesque style. To the east of it is the *House of Prayer* of the founder of the monastery. Near to St.

Finghin's church is one of the two round towers of Clonmacnoise: *O'Rourke's Tower*, nearly sixty feet high, with no dome, but eight windows. Two Celtic high crosses originate from the ninth century. The twelve foot high *Cross of the Scriptures* is dated as being from the tenth century. Several biblical motifs are depicted on it, including the Crucifixion and the Last Judgement. On the surrounding ground there are about 400 grave stones with Gaelic inscriptions. Despite this monastic complex being plundered and sacked 30 times, it was lived in until 1552. Only the English succeeded in driving the last inhabitants out of the monastery and the trading centre.

Cong ⑰. This little village tucked away to the north of Galway Bay is full of horror stories and legends about fairies and dwarves, benevolent spirits and headless giants. Back in the sixth century the village was a spiritual centre on the isthmus between Lough Mask and Lough Corrib. The Augustinian *Cong Abbey* dated from 1123 is left from that time, as a magnificent ruin. The sumptuous Processional Cross, which supposedly contains a fragment of the cross to which Christ was nailed, can be seen today in the National Museum in Dublin (see p. 148). On the shores of Lough Corrib is *Ashford Castle*, built in mock Tudor style in the eighteenth century, and now a luxury hotel.

Cork ⑱. The capital of the province of Munster is an important gateway for visitors, with its ferryport and international airport. This is a city of quick-witted, fast-talking charmers. The accent is flat and lilting, a little like the Welsh accent to which it is distantly related. Indeed, Cork's relations with Wales go back to its origins. Walsh (usually pronounced "Welsh") is still one of the most common surnames. The history of the town goes back to the sixth or seventh century, when St. Finnbarr founded a monastery here. With the vicissitudes of time, the settlement was overrun time and again, and sacked, and in 1690 even razed to the ground. Today Cork is an important cultural and economic centre in Southern Ireland, which besides an *Opera House* (1965), sports the tallest building in the country, the *County Hall*, with its 17 floors. This lively town, with its 25 bridges across the river Lee, rightly has an exceptional reputation for music: there are several music clubs, where jazz predominates; the *Jazz Festival*, which takes place every year in October, is well known all over Ireland.

In the Marsh, the historic town centre, are *the Church of St. Peter and St. Paul* built in 1868 in neo-Gothic style, brightly coloured 19th century houses, and around St. Paul and St. Patrick's Street are the shopping and business centres. The best known building, with its spires visible from far away, and delicate French Gothic cathedral style, is *St. Finbarr's Cathedral*, built between 1865 and 1880. Even if the name Cork itself (*Corcaight* in Irish Gaelic) means a marshy place, the place nevertheless has the lively charm of Mediterranean towns.

Croagh Patrick ⑲. Ireland's holy mountain (2500 ft) rises up directly from the coastal foreland to the east of Louisburgh. In 441 St. Patrick is believed to have fasted for

Left: The Celtic Irish were converted to the Christian faith in the fifth century. Early evidence of this christianisation is the twelfth-century Romanesque church of Kilmalkedar on the Dingle peninsula (top). From an even earlier period is the Gallarus Oratory, also on Dingle. The building, constructed almost entirely without mortar, is thought to be 1200 years old (centre). Another good example of the Irish Romanesque style are the portal and capitals of the Cong Abbey cloister (bottom).

Right: During the War of Independence between 1919 and 1921, the town of Cork was severely damaged. That is why hardly anything is left of the old building stock, and in many places gaps between buildings and wooden huts point to the wounds inflicted in the past. Nevertheless, Cork is a lively, attractive town, with an almost Mediterranean atmosphere. Bottom: The nets are still out to dry, but soon the fishing fleet on the Dingle peninsula will be going out again for the next catch.

40 days on the top of this cone-shaped mountain - following the example of Moses - to meditate, do penance and communicate with an angel. Here he is also supposed to have liberated the country from snakes. Nowadays, every year on the last Sunday in July, a major pilgrimage is held here, in which the faithful negotiate the stony path, some of them barefoot. The atmosphere during these climbs is relaxed and jovial, though.

Derry ⑳. The Northern Irish town of Derry, surrounded by the *town walls* which have been almost entirely preserved (from the early seventeenth century), has always been at the centre of the troubles. It is not just a matter of religion here, but social differences as well. The Catholics live west of the River Foyle; the Protestants live in the more prosperous Waterside, on the eastern bank. The town, which the Protestants call Londonderry, is the second largest in Northern Ireland, with its 65,000 or so inhabitants. In 1688-89 it withstood the 105 day siege by the troops of the Catholic King James II. William of Orange's troops had entrenched themselves in the town, to win Ireland for the Protestant cause. Derry is one of the oldest Irish settlements; a monastery was built on the river as early as 546. From the tower of *St. Columb's Cathedral* (built in 1633), with its melodious bells, there is a splendid view across the town and the nearby riverside area.

Dingle ㉑. Of the well-known "five fingers" which reach out into the Atlantic in the south-west of the island, the Dingle Peninsula is the most northerly, and the fishing village of the same name is the westernmost point in Europe, if one does not count Iceland. This restless, brightly coloured place is not just the destination of many coastal and deep sea anglers, but with its 1,500 inhabitants is also the largest settlement on the peninsula. This charming little town became famous not just because of its natural harbour, but also because of the many tourists who have felt themselves attracted as though by magic to this ancient Christian site, which can also look back on a long career as a smugglers' haven. The whole area of the peninsula is full of prehistoric and early Christian monuments. Particularly noteworthy is the *Brandon Mountain* (3,000 ft). According to legend, St. Brendan's hut was here, whence he sailed with 14 other monks to America in the eighth century. The seven-year adventure of these pious men was only chronicled 200 years later. Meanwhile, we know that Brendan certainly *could* have reached America by *island-hopping*, via the Hebrides, the Faeroes, Iceland and Greenland.

Donegal ㉒. The town originated from an earlier Celtic settlement, which the British revived in the early seventeenth century. Like the peninsula of the same name in the northern part of the island, this historical market town also belongs to the Gaelic-speaking area of Ireland. In the town, the fifteenth-century *Donegal Castle* stands as an impressive ruin, on a cliff over the banks of the river Eske. At the river mouth is the picturesque *Donegal Abbey*, built by the Franciscans in 1474. A monumental historical work was compiled within its walls between 1632 and 1636, the "Annals of the Four Masters", an epic on 3,000 years of Irish history. An obelisk, called *The Diamond*, stands as a monument to the authors, four Franciscan monks, in the diamond-shaped market square.

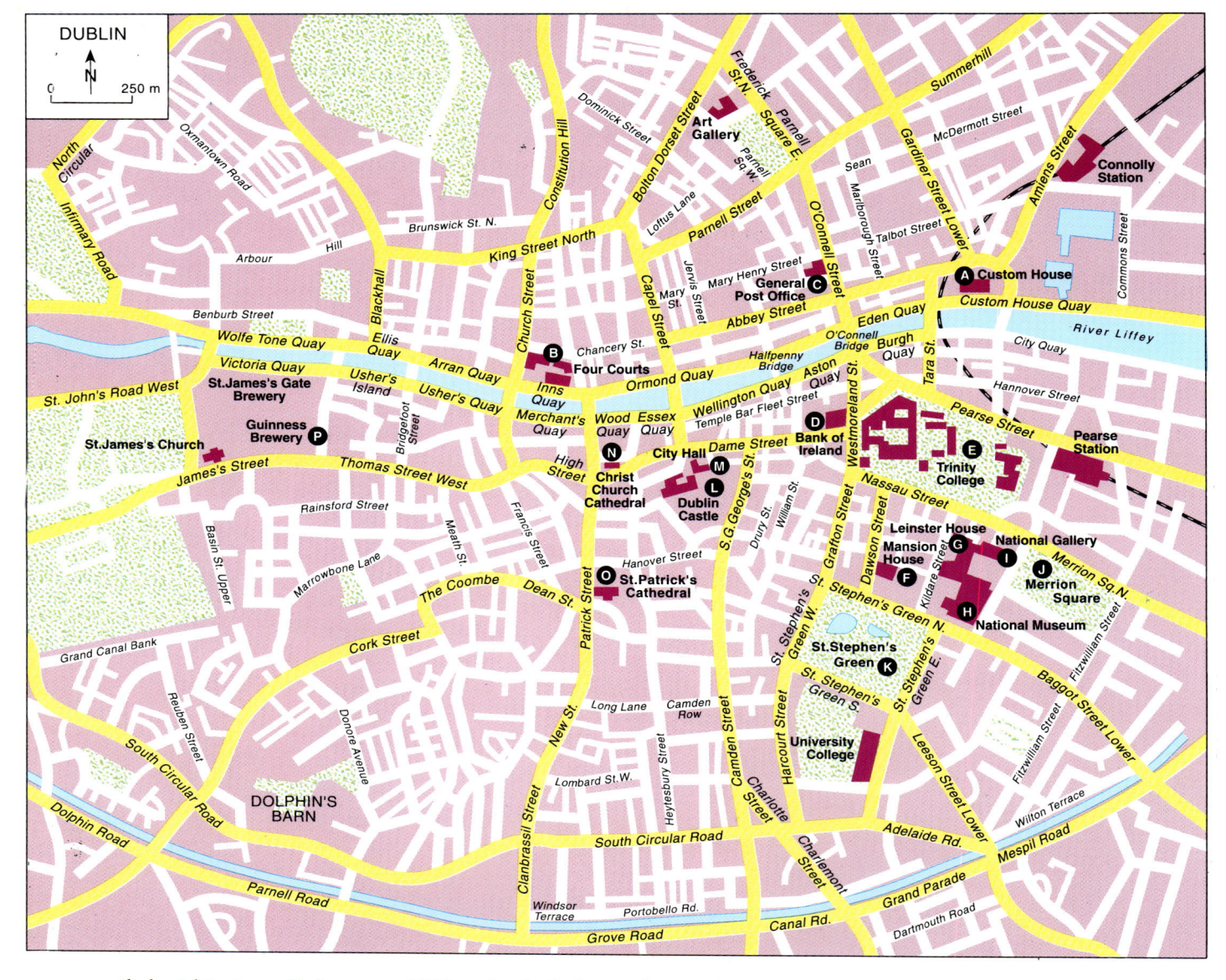

Dublin ㉓. The capital city of the Republic shows itself simultaneously as both proud and modest. It is by no means an ugly town, but neither is it altogether eye-catching, certainly not at first glance. The former Celtic settlement has been a cultural centre for the country ever since Celtic times. Today it has more than half a million inhabitants, and has developed into a lively centre of trade and administration, in which several light industries have located themselves, and not least the largest European brewery.

Very little survives of the original Viking settlement and not much of the medieval city. The two cathedrals, Christ Church and St Patrick's, both underwent extensive restorations in the nineteenth century, leaving them unrecognisable to those who knew them in their previous decayed but authentic state. Nearby, Dublin Castle likewise retains little of its medieval core. The historic city is almost all an eighteenth-century creation, the supreme achievement of the colonial Protestant Ascendancy. Although there are some good Victorian buildings and even some fine modern architecture - along with a lot of bad modern architecture - Dublin is basically a Georgian city.

Most of the tourist attractions are in the city centre, and you should get to know them on foot. The *Custom House* Ⓐ, a masterpiece built in 1791 by the architect James Gandon (1743-1823) in the Parisian style, has been restored. The Republicans set fire to it in 1921, and it was completely burnt out. From the same period and by the same architect is the *Four Courts* Ⓑ, which is the seat of the country's Supreme Court. The almost 450-foot long façade, with its Corinthian portico, is towered over by a dominant round structure with a dome. The *General Post Office* Ⓒ - from the same period as well - was the focal point of the Easter Rising in 1916 against British rule. In the hallway there is a memorial to the Irish patriots. Going along O'Connell Street, you come to the bridge of the same name, which is a good starting point for a walk around the city. From there you can reach both of Dublin's most impressive buildings, the *Bank of Ireland* Ⓓ, originally built as the

Parliament building in 1729, and *Trinity College* Ⓔ, the university founded by Elizabeth I in 1591. Passing through the 200-year-old portal, you come to a wide inner courtyard, and signposts direct you to the *Old Library*, built between 1712 and 1732, with its stock of around 5,000 old manuscripts and over two million books. There are some absolutely priceless treasures in the *Long Room*, a 200-foot long hall with a high wooden vault, which houses the "Book of Durrow" (seventh century), the "Book of Dimma" (eighth century), the "Book of Armagh" (ninth century), and last but not least the "Book of Kells" (ninth century), a richly decorated manuscript with the four gospels.

To the south of the university campus in Dawson Street, is the *Mansion House* Ⓕ, the mayor's residence since 1715, and in Kildare Street, which runs parallel is the magnificent *Leinster House* Ⓖ, built in Georgian style in 1745, and used as the Parliament building since 1922. The building is flanked by the *National Library* and the *National Museum* Ⓗ. The National Museum houses Ireland's most comprehensive and valuable collections from the country's early history, and the most valuable artefacts from the Bronze Age and the Early Christian period, including the Tara brooch, the Ardagh Chalice and the Cross of Cong. The Hall, with musical instruments from the past, is worthy of a visit too. On the left behind Leinster House is the *National Gallery* Ⓘ. About 2,000 works of art from eight centuries of painters, such as Degas, Monet, van Dyck, Rubens, Turner, Rembrandt, Michelangelo, Titian, Tintoretto, Goya, El Greco, Murillo, Zurbarán and many others, make this collection of paintings one of the finest in Europe.

Immediately to the east of this is the second largest square in Dublin, *Merrion Square* Ⓙ, built in 1762. On three sides of the square the façades are of uniform style. Oscar Wilde used to live at Number 1. The largest and the oldest square in the town is *St. Stephen's Green* Ⓚ, about nine hectares in size, with magnificent gardens, ponds, and several monuments. Between St. Stephen's Green and College Green, Grafton Street is the shopping centre. Smart pedestrian precincts, covered passage ways, boutiques and department stores have located themselves there. There is a colourful mixture here of students, shoppers and street musicians. Grafton Street and its adjacent streets are the most fashionable part of the city. About half-way along Grafton Street is the well-known "Bewley's" coffee-house, and in Harry Street is "McDaid's", the literary pub of the 'forties.

Dublin Castle Ⓛ stands out in the historical heart of the city. It is very likely that there was first a Celtic, and then a Danish fortress here, before King John had a castle built here in the thirteenth century. In the course of its history it has been renovated many times. The present building originates from the eighteenth century and is used for official State receptions. Immediately adjacent to it is the *City Hall* Ⓜ, which was built between 1769 and 1779 as the Royal Exchange. The old city of Dublin extends between Temple Bar and the Liffey. A few years ago the run-down old quarter was to be pulled down, but in the meantime the "Temple Bar lives" redevelopment project was started, with millions of punts allocated from the European regional

A view of the Dublin Custom House. From the opposite side of the river Liffey, the structure of the building can be seen to best effect, with its Doric portico and the 125 foot high dome in the centre.

development fund. Not far from the castle and the City Hall, *Christ Church Cathedral* Ⓝ towers up from the surrounding rows of houses. The cathedral originates from the eleventh century, though the present day church was rebuilt, in Gothic style, in the second half of the nineteenth century. The second Anglican church is the fourteenth-century *St. Patrick's Cathedral* Ⓞ. The inside of Ireland's largest cathedral, the national cathedral of the Church of Ireland (Anglican), is decorated with several mementoes from the days of the British Empire, and documents most impressively the Protestant domination of a Catholic country. Jonathan Swift, the author of *Gulliver's Travels*, who was Dean of the cathedral from 1713 until his death in 1745, is buried here. Behind both the cathedrals is the oldest part of the town, the Liberties. The area around Thomas St., Francis St., and Meath St. is one of the poorest in the city. A bitter-sweet smell of brewery mash hangs around in the air here. Guinness brews its "black beer" in the *St. James' Gate Brewery* Ⓟ.

On the north-eastern edge of the city is the wealthy suburb of Howth with its yachting harbour, castle and park. From here there is a splendid view over Dublin Bay, as far as Dun Laoghaire. On the south-eastern corner, near Dun Laoghaire, is Sandycove. The James Joyce Museum has been located in the Martello tower, where the author's letters, photos and personal effects are on display.

Ennis ㉔. This town on the Fergus River, with its 6,000 or so inhabitants, is the administration centre for Co. Clare, in the west of Ireland. The town centre, with its narrow, crooked streets, is best explored on foot. In so doing you cannot miss the Franciscan *Ennis Friary*, founded in 1241, but which the monks left in 1692, and it did not come under their guardianship again until 1969. Not far from the friary is the *De Valera Museum*, which has a library attached to it. Displayed here are documents about Ennis and its environs, as well as on the history of the whole island. Equally interesting is the *Craggaunowen Project*, an open air museum, which most impressively shows how people lived from the Bronze Age until the late Middle Ages.

The Trinity College buildings are in a large public park. Catholics were not admitted to study there until 1873.

Galway ㉕. Almost all visitors feel attracted by the atmosphere of this typically Irish town in the west. This port and industrial town on Lough Corrib, with a population of 38,000, is the centre for folk music, theatre and poetry in the west of Ireland. Maintaining and extending use of the Gaelic language is obviously a priority in this university town. Galway was first granted its town charter in 1484, but its history goes back to 1124, when a fort was built here. The sixteenth-century *Lynch's Castle* is a reminder of the influential Lynch family, which provided the town with several mayors between 1485 and 1654. The expression "Lynch law" is attributed to one of the Lynch family, when as mayor he sentenced and executed his own son for murder.

Giant's Causeway ㉖. In the north of the island, this is one of the most beautiful and impressive sights which the Irish coastline can offer. The extraordinary rock formations arose after tertiary volcanic eruptions, when the viscous basalt solidified into nearly 40,000 polygonal pillars. For many Irish, however, these basalt pillars, up to 80 feet high, are the work of the giant Finn McCool, who wanted to make a bridge across to Scotland.

View of O'Connell Bridge, Dublin. It is named after the man who is regarded as the founding father of modern independent Ireland.

Glendalough ㉗. Barely 40 km south of Dublin, in the heart of the Wicklow Mountains, is Glendalough, the valley of the two lakes, with its famous monastic settlement. The building goes back to St. Kevin, who withdrew here in solitude as a hermit, but attracted so many disciples, that he founded a monastery. After his death in 618, the centre was just at the beginning of its heyday. One of its best known abbots was Laurence O'Toole, who became Archbishop of Dublin in 1163. He is one of the few Irishmen who were officially canonised by Rome. *St. Kevin's Church* can claim ancient origins, as there was probably a burial ground here back in the Stone Age. Because of the chimney-shaped bell tower, the chapel is also wrongly called "Kevin's kitchen". The rectangular "Church on the rocks", which stands on a man-made platform *(Teampull na Skellig)*, can only be reached by boat. On the monastery land is also one of the best preserved round towers in Ireland. It is 100 feet tall and is five feet in diameter at the base, and has been maintained in original condition right up to the rooftop.

Glengarriff ㉘. Magnificent, fabulous, colourful and rich in flowers, is how this town in the south west is best described. Protected as it is by the Caha Mountains, and washed by the warming Gulf Stream, this village with its 300 or so inhabitants is more reminiscent of Tenerife than a rugged island in the Atlantic. Luxuriant plant life suggestive of the tropics, with yew trees, fuchsias, holly, rhododendrons, geraniums and roses, covers the rocky cliffs down to the sea. You can go across to *Garinish Island* by boat. On the island there are particularly beautiful gardens laid out with magnolias, camelias, and several exotic plants. The Glengarriff coast, with its innumerable small islands, is reminiscent of the Stockholm Archipelago.

"Dublin can be heaven ... there is magic in the air". Open air concert in Powerscourt Town Centre, near St. Stephen's Green.

Kells ㉙. About a thousand years ago, this market town with a population of barely 3000 was one of the pinnacles of Irish spiritual life. The place was known worldwide because of its manuscript gospel "Book of Kells", produced here in the ninth century. It can now be seen in the Trinity College Library, Dublin (see p. 149). A facsimile is on display in Kells, however, in *St. Columba's Church*, which is regarded as one of the oldest Protestant church foundations in Ireland (1578). Of the earlier monastic settlement, one round tower, a House of Prayer, and indeed five high crosses have been preserved, with these latter depicting scenes from biblical history. The best known, showing the miraculous distribution of the loaves of bread, is in the market place. From time to time it was used as a gallows.

Kilkenny ㉚. Its crooked streets and lanes give this town in the south east of the island a breath of medieval quaintness. *Kilkenny Castle* can be seen from a long way away; the oldest parts of it go back to the thirteenth century. The castle on the Nore River was used from 1391 until 1935 as the seat of the Butler family. This not exactly aristocratic sounding family name is derived from the honorary title of the noble family - they were head butlers to the king and were granted the privilege of importing wine. The magnificent castle building suggests that this trade was a lucrative one. In the group of buildings opposite the *Kilkenny Design Workshops* are now housed. Excellent artefacts are designed here, and in part manufactured as well. *Rothe House*, a merchant's house built in the Elizabethan style in 1594, with two courtyards one behind the other (now the offices of the Archaeological Society), and the *Court House* from 1794, are also worthwhile places for a visit.

Worthy of special mention is *St. Canice's Cathedral*, one of the most beautiful cathedrals in Ireland, from the thirteenth century. There are many beautiful tombs here, the oldest one for Henry de Ponto (1285), with delicate work in the black Kilkenny marble.

over 200 years ago; it goes back to the entertainment of "rounds". Edward Lear first drew attention to it in his *Book of Nonsense* in 1846.

First founded by the Vikings in the ninth century, this fourth largest town in Ireland with a population of 70,000, is today first and foremost a modern industrial town full of action and a lot of traffic, because it is here that the last bridges over the Shannon are, before it widens out into the estuary. Especially worth a visit is *King John's Castle* (thirteenth century), which is a pentagon-shaped defensive building with a main building, three round corner towers, a bastion and a two-tower gate structure. *St. Mary's Cathedral* can be particularly impressive with a fantastically carved choir bench made of oak (1489). Rare individual artefacts from the Bronze Age are kept in the *Hunt Museum*.

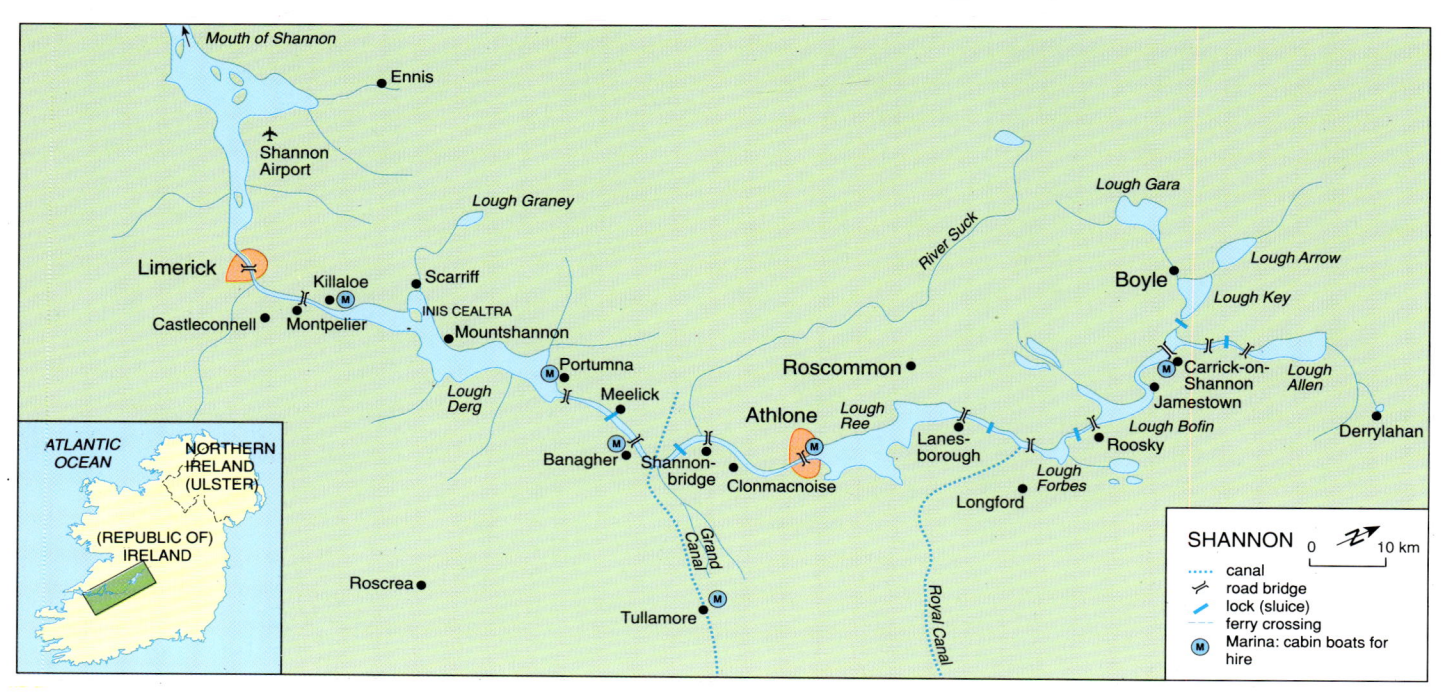

Kinsale ㉛. This prosperous small market town in Co. Cork, at the mouth of the river Bandon, is known for its gourmet restaurants and is a favourite destination for angling enthusiasts. From 1602 this little town with its population of about 2,000 was an English town - the Irish were not allowed to live here until the end of the eighteenth century. At that time the English built the town as a fortress. *Charles Fort* (1677) at Summer Cove, which overlooks Kinsale Harbour from the eastern bank, and was still in use until 1922, is a reminder of that time. The most remarkable building in the town, however, is the twelfth-century *St. Multose's Church*. The tower with the Romanesque portal, and inside the church a group of tombs (seventeenth century), and a baptismal font, are particularly impressive.

Limerick ㉜. This town at the beginning of the Shannon estuary is considered to be the place where "limericks" originated; these are humorous five-line stanzas, based on the following pattern: the first two lines introduce the subject matter, the next two reduce it to absurdity, and the fifth contains the punch-line. This form of verse was known

Monasterboice ㉝. Near the east coast of Ireland, ten kilometres north west of Drogheda, is the area of a former monastery building. This is where St. Buithe founded an abbey around 500, which only existed until the early twelfth century - after a fire in the round tower in 1097, in which the library was destroyed. Two churches, one round tower, two early gravestones, a sun-dial and three impressive high crosses - *Muiredach's Cross, Tall Cross* and the *North Cross* - have survived, however. These crosses depict scenes from the Old and New Testaments.

Newgrange ㉞. The neolithic burial ground near Drogheda, estimated at between 4500 and 5000 years old, is the most beautiful and most impressive long grave in the whole of western Europe. Jointly with the passage graves at Knowth and Dowth it is part of the largest burial site in the fortress on the Boyne (Brugh na Boinne), the area in the river valley of the Boyne being about three miles long and two miles wide. Newgrange is the largest of the three burial sites. It is a roughly heart-shaped stone and earthwork hill about 300 feet in diameter, and just about

BEING A PLEASURE BOAT SKIPPER ON THE SHANNON

The Shannon is the longest river in Britain and Ireland and together with its tributaries it drains over 15,000 square kilometres or more than 20 per cent of the entire island. It is commonly thought of as the great natural divider between the East and West of Ireland. While this is true in one rather obvious sense - crossing the great river has a dynamic quality to it which makes you feel that you are moving between two very different places - in another it is not. The western province, Connaught, lies on both sides of the river and had even more of its territory, about one-third in all, on the eastern shores in medieval times. However, the thing to do is not to cross the river but to sail on it. It is the great watery spine of Ireland. The source of the Shannon itself is at Derrylahan, Co. Cavan, and it disgorges into the sea at Limerick.

The Shannon region's reputation does not rest just on its watery landscape, but also on the picturesque beauty of the lakeland area. The river winds with several meanders through small, brightly coloured villages, broad fields of flowers and meadows, past castle ruins and wooded hills. There has been constant coming and going here throughout the centuries. The Vikings came along here pillaging with their dragon-headed longboats, the Irish and the British have fought over the strategically important region, and pilgrims have hoped for miracles. And still the flow of the curious does not diminish. Today the needs of a leisure society are reflected here with the place now a mecca for surfers, anglers, temporary boat skippers and nature-lovers. Anybody wanting to hire one of the 450 or so boats for hire, must satisfy two conditions: to be at least 21 years old, and that there will be two persons on board who are able to operate the boat. No pilot's licence for the waterway is required. The owner gives the necessary instructions, and then the temporary skipper can depart from the ports of Athlone, Portumna, Carrick-on-Shannon, or Killaloe with his cabin-cruiser. The craft are simple to navigate, and a Shannon cruiser will not do any more than 5 knots.

The journey from Limerick to Killaloe is historically interesting and attractive, and is full of surprises. At the port of Portumna begins Lough Derg - the largest lake on the Shannon at 24 miles long and up to 3000 feet wide. The most frequented stretch here is the one between Mountshannon and Scarriff. The Falls of Doonas at Castleconnell attract people as does a holy island. A monastery founded by St. Caimin was built in the eighth century on Inis Cealtra, and the ruins are still visible. This enjoyable way of discovering Ireland, above all, opens up insights into nature along the river. Nobody could possibly forget the scene, watching the steep river banks at sundown, with the sheep standing out as dark silhouettes on the grass.

There is hardly anything more therapeutic than a relaxing journey in a cabin cruiser along the Shannon, Ireland's longest river.

35 feet high. This hill was worshipped by the Celts as a divinity, the god of love. The lie of the grave is positioned precisely so that on 21 December, at the winter solstice, the rising sun shines in a straight shaft into the passage grave chamber, through a tiny aperture in the roof. Also famous is the megalith, in the entrance to the grave. The double and triple spiral motifs chiselled in leave no doubt about the care taken by the craftsmen. There was formerly a circle of megaliths around the hill, of which only twelve are still standing upright.

therefore has two cathedrals, both built in the nineteenth century. The town market place is dominated by an impressive twelfth-century high cross. Not far from here is the first industrial museum on the island, the *Mill Museum*.

About 1000 B.C. the legendary people *Tuatha Dé Danann* (the people of the goddess Danann) lived around Tuam. There are supposed to have been countless battles between members of this people, who were "large in stature, godlike, and masters of all the arts", and the people equally

One of the manor houses which is most worth visiting is Westport House in County Mayo. It was built by Richard Cassels between 1730 and 1734, and now houses an impressive collection of pictures. When visiting, one should certainly not miss the estate's water fountains in the park.

Sligo ㉟. This town on the river Garavogue in the north west of Ireland, documented for the first time in 537, attracts foreign students every July and August to the Yeats English Language School. The poet, William Butler Yeats (1865-1939) lived here for a while. He is buried in Drumcliffe village churchyard about 5 miles to the north. The town is to be recommended primarily as the starting point for enjoyable outings to the west and north. In the town itself the fifteenth-century Dominican *Sligo Abbey*, in which the choir dates from the time the abbey was founded (1253), is an impressive sight.

Tara ㊱. Just 25 miles north west of Dublin in the village of the same name is the *Hill of Tara*, a bare grassed hump, from which you can see far to the north and west. This is where the seat of the Irish chieftain kings used to be; they abandoned it in 1022. No trace is left of the former palace, in which about 140 kings are thought to have lived. Only earthworks overgrown with grass and graves testify to the former importance of the place.

Tuam ㊲. This was the seat of the last chieftain kings of Ireland, and once the most powerful town in the west of the country. Today, this town with a population of about 4,000 is the episcopal see for both major churches and

surrounded by legend, the Firbolgs (or Belgae, as they were called by Irish chroniclers). The remains of the ring fort near the village of Dunmore to the north east date back to that era.

Waterford ㊳. The symbol for this town in south eastern Ireland, founded by the Vikings in 853, is *Reginald's Tower*. This solid, round fortress tower was built around 1003, was used for a long time as a prison, and today houses the Waterford Museum. This port on the river Suir, with its 40,000 inhabitants, has been famous for its glass industry since the eighteenth century.

Westport ㊴. This small port in the north west of Ireland, situated among the most luxuriant vegetation, has in recent years devoted itself entirely to sporting anglers, as Clew Bay is an ideal stretch of water for fishing. Just three stone vaulted bridges cross over the river Carrowbeg, whose banks are fringed with trees. *Westport House*, built between 1730 and 1734, is of architectural interest. The seat of the Marquis of Sligo, it is now open to visitors. In the park there are wonderful fountains, which are operated by making use of the tidal flow. At the end of July, Westport is the starting point for pilgrims making their way to Croagh Patrick, the Holy Mountain of the Irish.

IRELAND

- ✝ Abbey, monastery
- ⬛ Fortress / Castle
- ⋯ Archaeological sites
- ★ Natural beauty spot
- ▲ Mountain

0 — 25 km

North Channel

ATLANTIC OCEAN

Bloody Foreland · FANAD PENINSULA · Malin Head
ARAN ISLAND · Malin · Culdaff
Portnoo · ★ GLENVEAGH NATIONALPARK · Milford · Buncrana · Greencastle · Portrush · ★ Giant's Causeway ❻ Ballycastle
Ardara · Letterkenny · Ramelton · Grianan of Aileach · Coleraine
Killybegs · Donegal · ❷⓪ Derry (Londonderry)
Donegal Bay · ㉒ · Stranorlar
Ballycastle · Bangor · NORTHERN IRELAND
Sligo ㉟ · Omagh · Lough Erne · Lough Neagh · Larne
❶ ACHILL ISLAND · Keel · Ballina · Enniskillen · ❽ Belfast
Mulrany · Lough Conn · ❺ · Armagh ❹
Clew Bay · Newport · Castlebar · Charlestown · Boyle ❾ · Downpatrick
Westport ㊴ · Ulster Canal · Newry
Kylemore Abbey ✝ · ⓳▲ Croagh Patrick · Leenane
Clifden · Cong ⑰ · Claremorris · Cavan · Dundalk
⑭ · Ballinrobe · Suck · Longford · Castlepollard · Kells ㉙ · Dundalk Bay
Oughterard · Tuam ㊲ · Roscommon · Lough Ree · Royal Canal · Monasterboice ㉝
❸ ARAN ISLANDS · Cashel Bay · Galway ㉕ · Athlone · Mullingar · Trim · ㉞ Drogheda · Newgrange
Cliffs of Moher ★ · Ballyvaughan · Kinvara · ⑪ Burren · Clonmacnoise ⑯ ✝ · Tara ㊱
⑮ · Lisdoonvarna · Shannon · Grand Canal · Tullamore · Maynooth · Malahide · Howth
Lahinch · Corofin · Lough Derg · Roscrea · Naas · ㉓ Dublin
Kilkee · Ennis ㉔ · Kildare · Enniskerry
Kilrush · Bunratty Castle ⑩ · Bray
Mouth of the Shannon · Tarbert · Shannon · Carlow ⑫ · Glendalough ㉗ · Wicklow
Clogher Head · Adare ❷ · Limerick ㉜ · Tipperary ⑬ · Kilkenny · Arklow
Dingle ㉑ · Tralee · Cashel ㉚ · Barrow
Dingle Bay · Killorglin · Kilmallock · Clonmel · Suir
★ Skellig Rocks · Cahirciveen · Killarney · Kanturk · Blackwater · ㊳ Waterford · Wexford
Waterville · Kenmare · Macroom · Youghal · Rosslare · Rosslare Harbour
❷⑧ Glengarriff · Bandon · ⑱ Cork
Black Ball Head · Bantry Bay · ❼ Bantry · Skibbereen · ㉛ Kinsale
Mizen Head

St. George's Channel

Index

Figures in italics refer to pictures

Index of Proper Names

Beckett, Samuel *81,* 84, 148
Behan, Brendan *81,* 84
Boru, Brian 10, 12
Burgh, Richard de 131

Columbus, Christopher 18
Cromwell, Oliver 15, 75, 125, 132

Elizabeth I, 61, 131, 149
Engels, Friedrich 62

Flaherty, Robert 133
Friel, Brian 84

Gandon, James 148
Gregory, Lady Isabella Augusta 84
Grimm, Jacob 83
Grimm, Wilhelm 83
Guinness, Arthur 37

Henry II 15, 37
Henry VIII 131

Jackson, Andrew 18
James II, 75, 76, 152
King John 149
Joyce, James 62, *80,* 84

Kennedy, John F. 18
King, Edward 136
Küttner, Karl Jacob 83

Law, Bonar *14*
Lear, Edward 152

MacMurrough (Clan) 15
MacSweeney (Clan) 130
Milton, John 136

Nixon, Richard 18
O'Brien, Flann 84
O'Brien, Counts of Thomand 136
O'Brien, Kate 84
O'Casey, Sean *81,* 84, 148

O'Connell, Daniel 128
O'Connor, Frank 84
O'Malley, Grace 82, 131
O'Rourke (Prince) 15
O'Toole, Laurence 151

Patrick, Bishop of Ireland 12
Ptolemy 131

Reagan, Ronald 18
Robinson, Tim 132
Robinson, Mary 64, 104

St. Brendan 42
St. Buithe 152
St. Ciaran 145
St. Finnbarr 146
St. Kevin 151
St. Patrick 64, 77, 133, 146, 147
Shaw, George Bernard *80,* 84, 148
Sheridan, Richard B. 148
Swift, Jonathan *81,* 84, 148, 150
Synge, John Millington 133

Tone, Wolfe 133

Valera, Eamon de *15*
Venedey, Jacob 83
Voght, Caspar van 83

Wilde, Oscar 63, *80,* 148, 149
William of Orange (William III) 75, 76, 125, 131, 147

Yeats, William Butler *80,* 84, 154

Index of Places and Topics

Aasleagh Waterfalls *103*
Achill Island 51, 82, *109, 110/111, 112, 124,* 126, 131, *132*
- Achill Sound 83, 131
- Atlantic Drive 82, 131
- Dooega 51, 131
- Killdownet Tower 131
Adare *2/3, 4/5*

Agriculture 105
Aillwee Cave 145
American War of Independence 15
Antrim Coast 130, 135, 136
Aran Islands 51, 108, 132, 133, 145
Ardara 130
Ards Forest 130
Armagh 77, 133
- Observatory 133
- Planetarium 133
- Public Library 133
- St. Patrick's Cathedral 133
Athlone 125
- Athlone Castle 125
Atlantic Ocean 11, 101, 102, 126, 128, 130, 145

Balladen 61
Ballina 125, 126, 133
- Moyne Abbey 126, 133
- Rosserk Friary 133
Ballinasloe 108, 134
Ballycastle 108, 125, 126, 128, 130, 135
Ballyliffen 130
Ballyporeen 18
Ballyshannon 130
Ballyvaughan 127, *128,* 145
Bangor 125, 126
Bantry 135
- Bantry Bay 133, 135
- Bantry House 135
- Whiddy Island 135
Barden 102
Beehive Huts 128
Beehive tombs 42
"Bed and Breakfast" 59, 108
Belfast 75, 102, 128, 130, 135, 136, *136*
- Albert Memorial Tower 136
- Botanical Gardens 136
- City Hall 135
- Queen's Island 135
- Queen's University 136
- St. Anne's Cathedral 135
- Ulster Museum 136
- Ulster Folk Park *142, 143*

Bilingualism 18, 104
Blackwater Bridge 128
Bloody Foreland 130
"Book of Armagh" 149
"Book of Dimma" 149
"Book of Durrow" 12, 149
"Book of Kells" 12, 64, 149, 151
Boyle 136
- Boyle Abbey 136
Boyne, Battle of the, 76, 152
Bray 125
Buncrana 130, 131
Bunratty Castle *85,* 136
- Bunratty Folk Park *92, 135,* 136
Burren 42, 101, 127, 128, 132, 136
Burren River 145
Buttevant 134

Caha Mountains 135, 151
Cahirciveen 128
Carlow 145
- Browne's Hill 145
- Carlow Castle 145
- Court House 145
- St. Patrick's College 145
Carndonagh 131
Carrantuohill 101
Carrick 130
Carrickfergus 130
- Carrickfergus Castle 130
Carrick-on-Shannon *6/7, 10, 67*
Casla 126
Cashel 108, 125, 145
- Dominican Church 145
- Quirke's Castle 145
Castlebar 125, 126
Castlecove 128
Castlepollard 125
Castlerea 125
Catholics 35, 75, 76, 147, 150
Catholic Church 64, 75, 84, 102
Cavan 66
Celts 12, 84
Celtic Culture 75, 104, 131
- Clonalis House 125
Clara 125
Clare 42, 136, 150

Clifden 17, 125, 126, 145
Cliffs of Moher *89,* 127, 128, 145
- Hag's Head 145
- O'Brien's Tower *89,* 145
Climate 101, 102
Clonmacnoise 145, 146
- House of Prayer 145
- Cross of Scriptures 146
- Cathedral 145
- O'Rourke's Tower 146
- St. Finghin's Church 145
Coleraine 128, 130
Cong 96, 125, 146
- Ashford Castle 146
- Cong Abbey 146, *146*
Connaught 102
Connemara 40, 42, 108, 125, 126, 145
Cork, 12, 102, 108, 134, 146, *147*
- County Hall 146
- Opera House 146
- St. Finbarr's Cathedral 146
- Peter and Paul's Church 146
Corofin *86/87,* 127
Corraun 131
Creaghanroe 77
Creeslough 130
Croagh Patrick 64, 126, 146, 147, 154
Cross of Cong 149
Cross of Moone 145
Crossmolina 126
Curlew Hills 136

Daire Domhain 42
Derry → Londonderry
Derrylahan 153
Dingle (Peninsula) *47,* 128, *128,* 134, *146,* 147
- Brendan Mountain 147
- Kilmalkedar *129*
Dingle (Town) *50,* 147
Doe Castle 130, *130*
Dolmen 145
Donagh Cross 131
Donegal (County) 17, 40, 42, 105, 108, 125, 130, 131, 147

Donegal (Town) 130, 147, 148
- Donegal Abbey 148
- Donegal Castle 148
- The Diamond (Obelisk) 148
Downpatrick Head 126
Drogheda 125, 152
Druiden 84, 125
Drumlins 125
Dublin (County) 101
Dublin (City) 12, *19,* 20 f, 38, 62 ff, *62, 63,* 66, 77, 84, 102, 108, 125, 134, 148 ff, 151
- Christ Church Cathedral 150
- City Hall 149
- Custom House 148, *149*
- Dublin Castle 149
- Four Courts 148
- General Post Office 148
- Halfpenny Bridge 62, 148
- Leinster House 104, 149
- Mansion House 149
- Merrion Square 149
- National Gallery 149
- National Library 149
- National Museum 146, 149
- O'Connell Bridge *19*
- Old Library 149
- St. Patrick's Cathedral 64, 150
- St. Stephen's Green 149
- Temple Bar 63, 149
- Trinity College *22,* 23 f, 63, 64, 65, 149, *150,* 151
Dun Laoghaire 125, 150
Dunluce Castle 130, *144*

Economy 42, 77, 102
Emigration 15, 17, 18, 51, 75, 102, 105, 126, 146
Ennis 85, 127, 128, 150
- Craggannowen Project 150
- De Valera Museum 150
- Ennis Friary 150
Enniskerry 125
- Powerscourt House 125
European Community 39, 77, 104

Fair Head 135
Fairies 161

Famine 18, 102, 126
Fanad Peninsula 130
Fermanagh 77
Festivals 108
Fishing 42, 64, 66, 77, 105, 126, 136
Fish stocks 64, 101, 105, 108, 133
Folk Music 61, 108, 150
Foreign Traffic 17, 51, 105, 108, 157
Foynes 37
French Revolution 15, 133
French Revolutionary Army 133, 135
Freagh 128

Gaelic Language 18, 83, 104, 125, 128, 132, 148, 150
Galway (County) 105, 150
Galway (Town) 108, 125, 150
- Lynch's Castle 150
Galway Bay 132, 136, 146
Garinish Island 17, 151
Giant's Causeway 77, 101, 128, 130, 135, *139,* 150
Glen Bay 130
Glencolumbkille 130, *131*
Glendalough *29, 34,* 108, 125, 151
- "Church on the Rock" 151
- St. Kevin's Church 151
Glengarriff 151
Glen Head 130
Glenveagh National Park 130
Gulf Stream 101, 135, 151
Gorumna Island 126
Greencastle 131
Grey Abbey 125
Grianan of Aileach 130, 131
Guinness Brewery 39, 150
Guinness Stout 17, 37, 38, 64, 84, 108, 150
Gulf Stream 101, 135, 151

Handicrafts 108
High Crosses 42, 145, 146, 151
Hill of Tara 125
Hollywood 125

Hore Abbey 145
Horn Head 130
Horse Rearing 125, 134
Hospitality 16, 35, 51, 83
Howth 125, 150
- Howth Castle 125

Independence 16, 104
Industry 104, 105
Inishbofin 130
Inisheer 132, 133
Inishmaan 132, 133
- Church of the Canons 133
- Dún Conor 133
Inishmore 132, 133
- Arkyne's Castle 133
- Cliffs of Kilmurrey 132
- Dún Aenghus *88,* 132
- Dún Eochaill *88*
- Teampall Breachain 132
Inishowen 131
Irish cookery 108
Irish Republican Brotherhood 15
Irish Republican Army (IRA) 77, 102, 104

Keel 82, *100,* 125, 126
Kells 151
- St. Columba's Church 151
Kenmare *50, 51,* 128
Kerry *43,* 108
- Ring of Kerry 128
Kildare 125, 134
- Japanese Garden 125
Kilfenora 145
- Burren Display centre 145
- Kilfenora Cathedral 145
Kilkee 127, 128
Kilkenny 151, 152
- Court House 152
- Kilkenny Castle 151
- Kilkenny Design Shops 152
- Rothe House 152
- St. Canice's Cathedral 152
Killala 126
Killala Bay 133
Killarney 42, *51,* 128
Killarney National Park *50, 58, 106*

Killary Harbour 126
Killorglin 108, 128
Killybegs 130
Kilrush 127, 128
Kinsale 51, 128, 152
- Charles Fort 152
- St. Multose's Church 152
Kinvarra 127, 128, *128*
Kylemore Abbey 126, *126*

Lahinch *89*, 127, 128, 145
Lake District 66
Larne 128, 130, 135
Leenane 125, 126
Leinster 102
Letterkenny 130, 131
Lettermore 126
"Lia Fail" 125
Limerick 12, 85, 128, *129*, 134, 136, 152, 153
- Hunt Museum 152
- King John's Castle *129*, 152
- St. Mary's Cathedral 152
- Treaty Stone 152
"Limericks" 152
Liscannor 145
Literature 16, 83, 84
Londonderry 75, 77, 128, 130, 147
- St. Columb's Cathedral 147
- Town walls 147
Longford 125
Lough Conn 133
Lough Corrib 51, 146, 150
Lough Cullin 133
Lough Derg 66, *67, 74*

Lough Erne 77
Lough Foyle 131
Lough Key *70, 71,* 136
Lough Mask 126, 146
Lough Neagh 101
Lough Ree 125
Lough Swilly 130, 131
Louisburgh 146

Macroom 128
Magilligan Point 131
Maine River 42
Malahide 125
Malin Head 51, 130, 131
Maynooth 64
Mayo 17, 40, 66, 125, 126, 133
Megalith graves 42, 136
Middletown 37
Milford 130
Moate 125
Monasterboice *28,* 42, 152
Monks 12, 42, 75, 128, 147, 150
Mourne Mountains 125
Moville 130
Moy River 126
Moyne Abbey *see* Ballina
Muckish Mountain 130
Muff 131
Mulraney 126
Munster 102, 105
Music 35, 61

National Identity 16, 62, 104
National Symbols 104
Navan 125
Newgrange 42, 108, 125, 152

Northern Irish 38, 75, 76, 102, 108, 130, 131, 147
Northern Ireland Problem 77, 102
Nore River 151
Normans 12, 125, 145

Oughterard 125, 126
Ox Mountains 133

Parknasilla 128
Political System 102
Population 102
Portballintrae *77*
Portbradden *137*
Portnoo 130
Portrush 77, 128, 130, 135, *140/141*
Portstewart 77
Poulnabrone Dolmen 42, 128, 145
Protestants 35, 75, 76, 102, 147, 150
Pubs 11, 35 ff, *36, 37, 38, 39,* 62, 63, 64, 82, 84, 108

Rathmelton *117,* 130
Rathlin Island 135
Rathmullen 130
Reformation 75
Religious Wars 15
Ring Walls 42
River Fergus *86/87,* 150
River Foyle 147
River Lagan 135
River Lee 146

River Liffey *19,* 62, 64, 148, 149
River Moy 133
Rock of Cashel *10, 12,* 12, *13,* 145
- Cormac's Chapel 145
- St. Patrick's Cathedral 145
- Vicar's Choral Hall 145
Roscommon 125
Ross Beigh *43/44, 54*
Rosslare 108
Round Towers 42, 151

Scotland 77, 101
Shankill 125
Shannon (River) 66, *67,* 101, 108, 125, 128, 136, 145, 152, 153
Singing Pubs 61
Skelligs 41, 128
Skibbereen 35
Slea Head 128
Slieve League *102,* 130
Slievnae 128
Sligo 42, 154
Sneem *43, 46*
Songs 16, 40, 104
Spanish Point 128
Staigue Stone Fort *40, 54,* 128
Stone Age 40, 42, 132, 151
Story-telling tradition (Narrative tradition) 84
Strangford *76, 138*
Swilly, River 131

Tara 154
Tarbert 128

Tinkers 102
Tipperary 145
Tory Island 130
Tralee 38, 108, 128
Trim 125
- Trim Castle 125
Tuam 154
Twelve Bens 17, *98/99*, 145

Ulster 75, 102, 135
Ulster Defence Association 102
Ulster Volunteer Force 102
USA 15, 18, 42, 102, 105, 126, 134, 147

Ventry 128
Vikings 12, 125, 152, 153

Waterford 154
Waterville *52/53*, 128
Westport 125, 126, 154, *154*
- Westport House 154
Wexford 101, 108
Whiskey 37, 108
Whiskey distilleries 37
Wicklow 12, 125
Wicklow Mountains *8/9, 30,* 101, 108, 125, 151

Youghal 66
Youth Emigration Action Group 18

Picture Sources

Archives for Art and History, Berlin: p. 12, 80 (4), 81 upper (3)
Picture Archives of Prussian Cultural Heritage: p. 81 lower

Ringier Documentation Centre, Zürich: P. 78 upper
Walter Pfeiffer Collection, Dublin: p. 60 (6)
Axel Schenck, Bruckmühl: p. 62, 63 upper (2)
Süddeutscher Verlag (South German Publishing House)/Picture Library Munich p. 14(2), 15, 78 and 79
The copy of the dry point engraving on page 61 is reproduced with the kind permission of Mrs. Gertrude Degenhardt from her book *Farewell to Connaught!* Mainz, Edition GD 1987
The maps on pages 127, 148, 152, and 155 drawn by Astrid Fischer-Leitl, Munich

Text Sources

Hans Trausil: Irish Harp. Poems from the Eighth Century to the Present Day: Ebenhausen near Munich: Langwiesche-Brandt, 1983

We thank all copyright holders and publishing houses for permission to reproduce and copy. Despite intensive efforts on our part, it was however not possible to contact all copyright holders. Would those concerned please contact the publishing company.

Printing:

Design: Axel Schenck
Reader's Department: Angelika Franz, Christa Klus
Picture Documentation: Maria Guntermann
Graphics: Barbara Markwitz
Production: Angelika Kerscher

Technical Production:
Ressemann Photo Setters, Hochstadt;
Repro Ludwig, Zell-am-See, Austria
Printing: Grafedit S.p.A., Bergamo, Italy

Published in Ireland by
Gill & Macmillan Ltd
Goldenbridge
Dublin 8
with associated companies throughout the world

Copyright © 1994, 1995 by Verlag C. J. Bucher GmbH, München
English translation copyright © 1996 by Michael O'Mara Books Ltd
Introduction © 1996 by J.P. Donleavy
This edition published by arrangement with
Südwest Verlag GmbH & Co. KG, München

0 7171 2498 3

Photographs by Fritz Dressler and text by Siggi Weidemann
Published in Great Britain 1996 by
Michael O'Mara Books Ltd

All rights reserved. No part of this publication may be copied, reproduced
or transmitted in any form or by any means, without permission of the
publishers.

A CIP catalogue record is available for this book from the British Library.

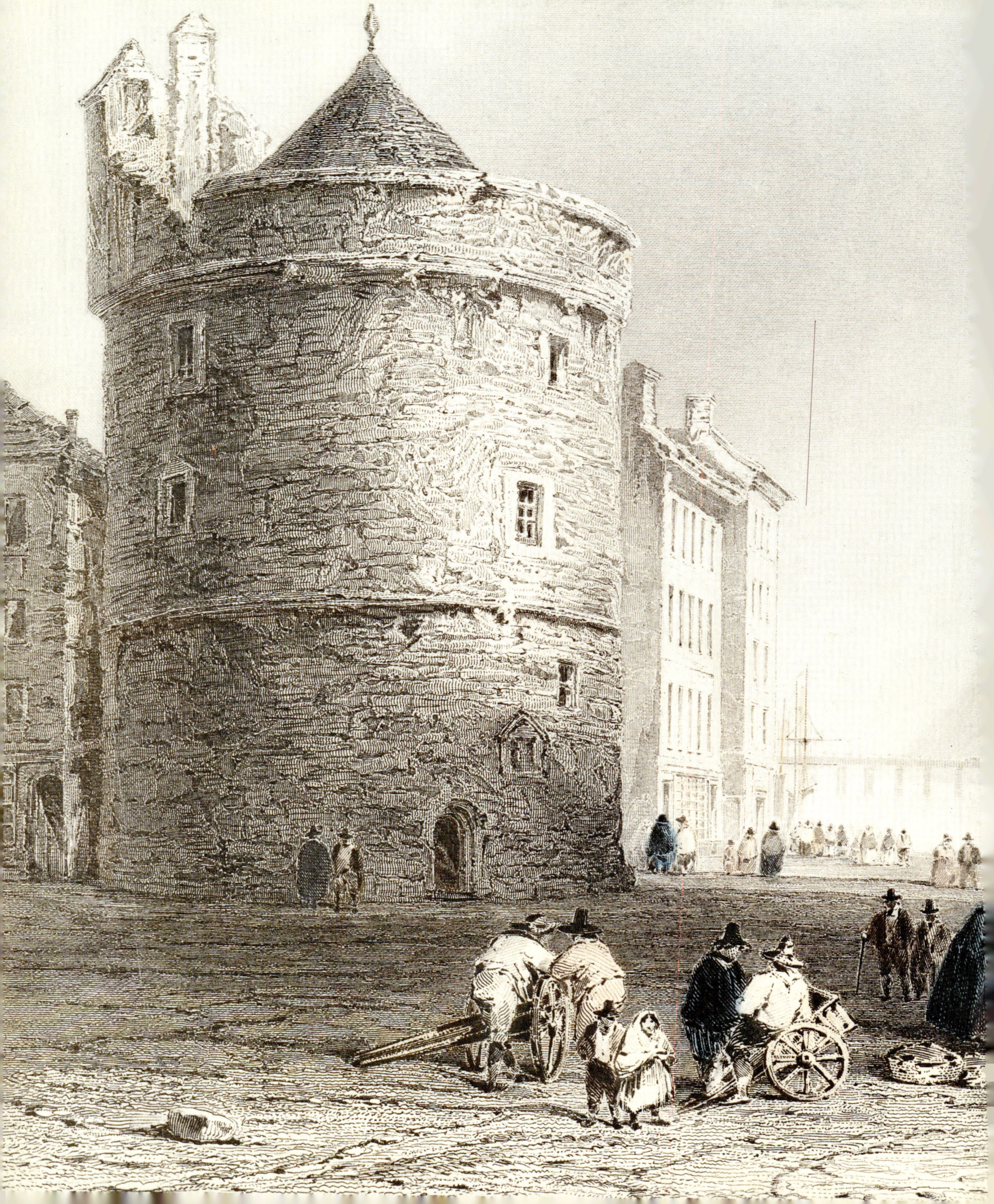